Screw the Business Plan

Screw the Business Plan

Screw the Business Plan

SCREW THE BUSINESS PLAN

MASTERING THE SKILLS AND MINDSET TO PROFIT FAST

Dr. Talonda Thomas

Cooley-Parks

Screw the Business Plan

Copyright © 2018,2023

by Talonda Thomas All rights

reserved.

Published in the United States by Cooley-Parks Publishing

ISBN-13: 978-1724300782

ISBN-10: 1724300784

Printed in the United States of America

Screw the Business Plan

For Malachi & Julien

CONTENTS

INTRODUCTION
YOU'RE ALL YOU'VE GOT 1

CHAPTER 1
DREAMS DON'T BUY THE CADDY 7

CHAPTER 2
MONEY GRUBBER 25

CHAPTER 3
THE MASTER OF MARKETING WINS 41

CHAPTER 4
PAY YOURSELF FIRST 55

CHAPTER 5
THE POWER OF MENTORSHIP 67

CHAPTER 6
BUILD RELATIONSHIPS THAT MATTER 74

CHAPTER 7
CREATING A WOW TEAM 84

CHAPTER 8
THE ART OF LIVING................................. 109

CHAPTER 9
PRODUCTIVITY 121

CHAPTER 10
WORK-LIFE BALANCE 128

CHAPTER 11
THE POWER OF AFFIRMATIONS, FAITH AND GRATITUDE..142

CHAPTER 12
LIVING FEARLESSLY................................. 155

CHAPTER 13
THE POWER OF PERSEVERANCE 161

CHAPTER 14
SCREW THE BUSINESS PLAN................... 171

CHAPTER 15
FAIL, BUT FAIL FAST 193

CHAPTER 16
**FULFILL YOUR DREAM WITH
INTEGRITY** 199

Screw the Business Plan

INTRODUCTION
You're All You've Got

Congratulations! The fact that you picked up this book means that you're a part of the small percent of the people who didn't just have an idea but decided to put your great ideas into action. Maybe you're unhappy with your current job or relationships and simply need a change. It could be that you've been fighting a feeling of boredom or the unsettled feeling in your gut that you're made for more, have more to give, and that you've been playing it way to small. If you know that you have something great to offer the world but are tired of getting stuck in the details, then this book is for you and will teach you the skills and mindset that you will need to survive your first years in business.

This book is part memoir and part business success secrets straight from the trenches about taking everything that's holding you back from getting your business off the ground to living life on your own terms. The concept of *Screw the Business Plan* isn't to encourage entrepreneurs not to plan wisely. Instead, I would rather you put a smart plan into action and learn the skills that'll thrust your dream off the shelf. You see, the typical entrepreneur is a dreamer and spends a lot of time thinking about great ideas, most of which never even make it to paper. We didn't just wake up this way. Most of us started this *wondering* about what we could achieve back in grade school.

2   *Screw the Business Plan*

I was one of those kids. Someone who wasn't quite positive in high school what I wanted to do, so I dabbled in different areas of work always knowing I could do the job better than my boss. I had some terrible bosses who made me dread each day and wake up wondering how much longer I would be forced to stay there dependent on them for every dollar. And even when I found a job I loved, I realized that they'd screw me over any chance they could (like many jobs). The pay would be *just* enough, and I was never left with an abundance to live the way my family deserved. Sound familiar?

For me, the reality check came about five years into my career as a sixth-grade public school teacher when a highly respected colleague of mine was accused of having sex with a student. He was removed from the school immediately, before any trial, and he was gone so fast the work gossip hadn't even begun. The details were *very* juicy. I listened to the news stories and gossip around the school with the same disbelief as everyone else, but my disbelief wasn't focused on the act of the school principal *getting it on* with the high school student. The entrepreneur in me couldn't help but wonder, "What if this guy didn't do this?" I mean, seriously, what if he was found innocent? As an entrepreneur, I've even had customers threaten to accuse their service provider of touching them inappropriately if their demands for a refund weren't met so I'm highly aware that some people lie. However, any male schoolteacher will let you know that it only takes one quick accusation, and you're gone. Regardless of my coworker's innocence or guilt, the money ran dry in my head the moment I realized that my employer could release me at any moment. At that very second, I realized my money would be gone as soon as my boss said so.

Screw that.

I need money that I can count, sniff, and pour across my bed while I roll around in it. Yes. All of that! The idea that someone could take away my paycheck makes me start to break out into hives. You see, I don't have a plan B. I *am* plan B. And if my family is going to eat, it's going to be because I hustle every day to make sure they have what they need and are not dependent on what someone else is willing to offer them. You, too, can take all the chips on the table and put them back where they belong. Into your own pockets.

If you believe you can launch a great business while teaching an audience of followers to pay you, and you *know* you've got the guts to get the job done (because that's what it's going to take), then I'd like to share with you some of the strategies I've learned through my experience and the stories of other very successful people over the years.

Put a little faith in yourself and get ready to count some cash with me.

SECTION I
Dream Chasing

Chapter 1
DREAMS DON'T BUY THE CADDY

Growing up with two middle-class parents, it was expected that good grades in school would be followed by a college degree and a reliable job with a pension. If there are two things I remember about my parent's professions, it was that my mother came home exhausted every day from being a high school teacher and my father spent most evenings on every side business that existed. He tried his hand selling Quorum International products, VitaMist Spray Vitamins, Isagenix, and there were talks of opening a bar (which, rumor has it, my mother put a quick stop to), and those are just the ones that I remember. Now that he is retired, he is on to selling real estate and filing income taxes for people.

For my dad, the grind was and still *is* real.

Like most parents, mine were completely different from one another and yet still amazing in very different ways. My mom was simply over the moon to make it off the farm of Mississippi and into a big, beautiful, new home built from the ground up. Yet my dad had entrepreneurial dreams that kept him up at night. Obviously, he'd met people along the way who were doing very well for themselves and saw that there was money to be made. The only problem is that dreams don't give you cash. As a result, my father worked a long and fruitful career with the local utility company, and his job paid for the beautiful Cadillacs that his dreams were unable to fund at the time.

Many people are just like my dad. They dream of success knowing that they only have to get it right once. The problem is that many people run out of steam while on their pursuit to greatness and have a hard time gaining momentum while life continues to send blow after blow. But I'd like you to consider some people who were met with hardship. Henry Ford of the Ford Motor Company exhausted every moment attempting to create something that no one else envisioned but was met with failure at every turn. Not only did his first two automobile ventures fail, but he spent years on the brink of bankruptcy. While people laughed and thought he was crazy, he continued toward his dream relentlessly even if it meant financial ruin.

Another dreamer who found a way to keep going was Thomas Edison who couldn't stop creating new inventions and yet couldn't seem to stop experiencing failures. His first business went bankrupt, several others failed, and he even experienced hearing loss in the process. Talk about having a tough time. But no matter how difficult things were, he only needed to get it right one time. And thank God he did because without his unwillingness to give up, we would never have the invention of the light bulb, record players, the motion picture camera, or electric power distribution. You too may be experiencing hurdles in your attempt to get your business off the ground or paying you what you deserve.

Reasons Why Dreamers Don't Get Paid

- Lack of money

- No exposure to other entrepreneurs

- Fear of financial failure

- Fear of sales and asking people for money

- Stalled on details, such as an incomplete website

- Jumping into a business you have no passion for

- Jumping into a business you know nothing about

- Focusing on the idea but taking little action

- Fear of not having a regular paycheck

Fear Becomes the Setback

I've never thought of myself as a perfectionist. I was barely a "B" student in school. However, an extended time in higher education taught me about the iterative process and that it's okay to keep working on something repeatedly in hopes of getting a better result. However, successful money movers don't need a college degree to know that the most important key to success is speed and fixing things as you go along. You can spend a weekend on a website or an hour trying to put together the perfect social media advertisement campaign, but you must be willing to press the **Go** button on it. Sometimes you've got to accept *good enough* to get decisions made and move on to other areas where you can start making money.

You can't spend a month making the perfect landing page.

By the time your URL goes live, your competitor is already eating up your cash. To survive in the high frequency and highly productive world of successful business owners, you've got to be willing to *pull the trigger*. Think about what's currently sitting on your desk or in your email. Are you working on the perfect business flyer? Have an email from a potential client or employee that you're not sure how to answer? Maybe it's even one of your kids who keeps asking for permission to do something, and you haven't made the decision. Do it right now. To move from ideas to action, you have to be concise and decisive. You're not always going to make the right decision or publish the perfect content. It doesn't matter.

Pull the trigger.

If you find your time is being eaten up creating content or on any task that is not one of your strong skill-sets, then you need to hire help. You don't have to look far and the right person might even happen to live with you. Some of the best advances in my business have been when I asked my kids for help. Children are more tech savvy and think more succinctly than most millionaires. They don't get lost in the details and neither should you. Get creative in finding the support needed to push you forward. It's often thought that successful people became successful because of inherited wealth or that they got lucky but this isn't true for most. What is true is that successful people do everything ethically possible and do not take "no" for an answer. Consider Benjamin Franklin who offered 50 people lifetime subscriptions to hire business for providing initial support or Walt Disney who lacked in funding to make his dreams a reality so he visited art schools to recruit young artists knowing that he couldn't afford an experienced team.

DAYMOND JOHN
FUBU

For many people, their products or big ideas are stuck in their imagination station. Daymond John is one of the unique entrepreneurs who voices his experience going from zero dollars to a multi-million dollar company. He is candid about the hardest part of starting FUBU—his ability to take the initial steps to get it up and running.

Unlike many dreamers who get to sit in front of a computer working on the perfect sales email, Daymond actually had to go through the actions of sewing his hats and then selling them for ten dollars a piece. He was able to see early on that people were clearly interested in his designs, but you can't make a living selling ten dollar hats while you're the designer, manufacturer, and customer service representative.

Daymond was smart. He had a job working at Red Lobster and used that to keep himself afloat while the dream was growing. Soon, he found a routine that worked. Instead of "getting to his business when he had time," it was a part of his daily routine.

Daymond would wake up around 7:00 a.m. to process and ship orders until the afternoon, head to work at Red Lobster around 4:00 p.m., and then come back home to make more hats to put out the next day. He'd be awake well into the midnight hours and back up early in the morning.

Daymond once said, "To the public, FUBU was a huge company. Little did they know that I was still serving them shrimp and biscuits!"

> It ain't easy to keep hustling to bring your dreams into reality, but John found something that he was passionate about and said, "You need to re-evaluate if your passion doesn't get you through the rough stages."
>
> Seeing how profitable this business could be, Daymond and his mother mortgaged their house for $100,000. Things took a turn for the better when Daymond brought a few friends on board.
>
> So, note—he had an idea. He started creating the products and selling them (making improvements as time went on). He kept employment to pay his bills while growing his business and proved himself worthy of financing. As the work got too busy to keep up with, he hired help and grinded until he realized that he could enjoy life a bit more with the rewards that his profits provided.
>
> The hustle has to be fierce and unrelenting until you've built your business up enough to enjoy the fruits of your labor. When your personal phone rings a little less and money is still rolling into your account, you'll know it's okay to relax a little more—but yet, always grind.

My story of funding my business is similar to Daymond's. After five years of teaching twelve-year-olds music, I cashed in on my credit cards and the little bit of money that I had in my 401k, and then took a leap. Signing a lease for a new commercial space meant that I couldn't sit on my butt and hope for the best. I had to be up late hours and again early in the morning making sure everything got done. I hired a friend to work for cheap the first year that we opened because it was mutually beneficial, and we continued to grow for five years before I finally left my job.

If you want to see this dream happen, you've got to find something that can keep you in love with the idea for a long time because you won't be able to give up on it. Everyone has resources, so think creatively about what you've got and most of all, who you've got. Start small and above all else, utilize your hours of the day just as meticulously as Daymond John did.

Wealthy people practice routines that create their wealth, keep their wealth safe, and then multiply it. This is going to require you to change the people who you hang around and this is the most difficult part. You can love you family, your best friend, and the people who you've been in the routine of calling, but reaching your next level of success is going to mean replacing the time you spend on this comfortable relationships with people who have what you want or have achieved what you want to achieve.

If you want to learn how to fix cars, you spend time with a mechanic. To learn how to be a barber, you learn from other barbers. If you want to learn how to play piano, you need a piano teacher. So why on God's green earth do people think that they don't need to spend time around people who have mastered the creation, attraction, and accumulation of wealth? Networking with other entrepreneurs is often the single most important ingredient missing in the money-making process.

Each month, I spend a handsome sum of money to work with a business coach. With this level of mentorship, I receive coaching calls several times a month, access to newsletters with strategies that work, along with access to a network of other entrepreneurs. even paying for me

Having access to groups of people who are walking the same path is immeasurable. The more money I make, the more I invest in higher level groups that put me in the room with multi-millionaires and billionaire. And believe me, the conversations are very different with people who understand how valuable each of their hours on earth are. Unless you come from wealth and have been taught how to achieve what you want, then you've got to take the time to learn from others and get past the fear that stops most people from ever seeing real success.

Fear can be a very real handicap for business owners. It can cripple you before you even begin. Fear can literally make people violently ill. Anything with that much power is a problem. There are thousands of people who have the resources and support around them to take their ideas to the next level, but it's still not enough.

As stated by Travis Kalanick, the co-founder of Uber "Fear is the disease. Hustle is the antidote." This statement is so true as fear is one of the biggest challenges new entrepreneurs face. You ask yourself constantly what could go wrong but our biggest fears rarely ever happen. If you've spent time around me, you may notice the tattoo on my left wrist that says *fearless*, as a reminder that I can do hard things and overcome the gut reaction to be afraid of change. Instead of letting fear slow you down, use it as an indicator that opportunity is close. What you do with that opportunity will be up to you.

Ever since most of us were kids, our parents taught us about getting good jobs and having a large savings account for rainy days. We have been programmed from such a young age to follow a particular path and warned that employment with a good company was the only way to keep our families fed. It's pretty darn hard to think about not working a day job when you've barely got enough money to keep the electricity on, even *with* a paycheck.

What I've found is that there's only one way to get past that, and it's to hustle until your body tells you that you couldn't do one more thing at end of the day.

Many people have a period when they test things out with a cushion of some sort. Maybe you are fortunate enough to have a spouse with a steady income, or you've been sitting on some investments for a while that you could cash out. You might even be working a part-time or even full-time gig at the moment. There's nothing wrong with holding on to all opportunities while you grow your business. In fact, the smartest thing that you can do is fund your own company until you get too big and must have access to more money to keep things growing. But most of all, understand that there will come a point when you have to put everything on the line to get a life of true freedom.

Recently, I talked with two hopeful entrepreneurs about their businesses and they both explained that they hate asking people to buy products. Both sold high quality products, but they were so wrapped up with their shame of asking people to pay them they forgot they're actually *helping* someone by asking them to make a purchase. Zig Ziglar once said that "timid salesmen have skinny kids", and I've learned this to be true. Your family and loved ones deserve to be comfortable and to know that you work hard to take care of those your love. You have an obligation to yourself and to those you love to show up believing in yourself and in the fact that what you sell serves others. Everything in life is sales. You were sold ideas when you went to school as a kid and your parents had to sell you on even walking into the school building. The grocery store sells you food that you need for nourishment and you always seems to buy your favorite snacks, clothes, that new iPhone, or the last purchase you made. You were sold each of these from the beginning.

Maybe we start to feel a bit squeamish about selling because our parents told us it was wrong to "beg people for money." At least that's what my mother always told me. Well, at some point you've got to let go of any uneasy feelings you've got about money and realize that *not asking* for the sale is equivalent to starving yourself. Even worse, you're starving your family.

Businesses become profitable when the business owner realizes that they need to get every sale, upsell, and find hidden sale so that they can eat better than their neighbor. Having a business is not about giving freebies, lowering your prices to make your friends feel more comfortable, or waiting for people to beg you to take their money. Owning your own business is about creating a great product or service, providing better customer service than everyone else, and providing a platform for people to spend their money at the most that you can charge. When you've mastered that, find a way to get them to spend more. Plan events and offer packages for your *high rollers* who get the thrill out of their ability to spend more than their friends. Don't think that these people don't exist. Many of them are your friends and *their* friends. Now collect your cash.

Jumping into a Business You Have No Passion For

We need to get this out of the way early. I am from the school of thought that there is a big difference between entrepreneurs and those simply wish to be their own boss. "Entrepreneur" by definition means a person who organizes and operates a business, taking on greater than normal financial risks in order to do so.

Someone who wants to work for themselves simply has seen that people are making money on the side, and they begin to think about how cool life would be without answering to a boss. Which one are you?

If you are not taking extreme financial and emotional risks in this process, then you probably are simply looking to make extra money and would be even *more* thrilled if you could retire early. This may give you enough motivation to get started but not to see your idea through until it's successful. To stick with it, you must have financial skin in the game and build a business that aligns with what you believe in. You should be a consumer of your own product or service so that theirs both passion and belief to fuel your perseverance. Starting and growing a business is often challenging and requires significant effort and dedication. When you are genuinely passionate about what they do, you'll be more likely to stay committed and overcome obstacles that come your way. Your passion becomes a source of inspiration and allows you to maintain the necessary drive to succeed, even in the face of setbacks.

Belief in the products and services you offer is essential for building trust and credibility with customers. Imagine owning a restaurant that you refuse to eat in or creating a beauty line but not using your own products. When entrepreneurs truly believe in what their providing, it reflects in the quality and value of their offerings. This genuine belief is contagious and can resonate with customers. When entrepreneurs are passionate about their products and services, they're more likely to invest the time and effort required to continuously improve and innovate so that their business can survive challenges.

Overall, building a business based on passion and belief not only provides the entrepreneur with personal fulfillment but also enhances the chances of long-term success. It drives motivation, resilience, and the genuine connection with customers, ultimately leading to a stronger and more sustainable business foundation. This doesn't mean to follow your passions and pursue businesses that don't prove they can provide long-term cashflow. It means to get behind something that you willing to commit to fighting for. If you don't have a product or service that you love or have spent time developing, it may never be worth fighting for.

Living on the Fence

Another reason that many people fail to get their businesses off the ground is because they keep dipping their toes into the water of entrepreneurship, never really diving in with everything to lose. People who still have their 401ks, great earnings from their full-time jobs, and haven't put any collateral up for their businesses operate on a totally different frequency than the business owner down the street who must make a profit to avoid telling his son he's got to come home from college cause the tuition bill can't be paid.

Jeff Bezos lived life on a tight budget while building Amazon. Oprah worked without pay and refused to give up. Mark Cuban worked as a bartender until his business took off and Sara Blakely invested her entire life savings of $5,000 to start Spanx. You have to be willing to do anything and everything ethically possible to succeed. I'm not telling you to run to the bank for a business loan or to put your house up for collateral. No. But you've got to find some way over the fence of fear and, most of all, uncertainty. Deciding whether you want to be an employee or employer should be based on your passion and what type of leadership roles you're prepared to assume. As long as you are an employee, you're just a number.

You are what someone else can afford. When you were hired at your last job, the company brought you in because they needed someone to do the labor. The head boss could not or would not do the work and had enough money to pay you to do it. Whatever amount of money that you help the company make, you get a cut and the top boss gets a cut. Don't worry too hard about trying to figure out the math. I promise, the company made much more of that money than you did but that's because it costs to run a business.

My Final Seven Days of Employment

It was a Thursday morning, and I wasn't feeling so much at ease. I'd been planning all year on telling my boss **tomorrow** that I was quitting. My resignation letter had been saved on my computer desktop for more than six months, but the anxiety of having to actually let the words out my mouth *after ten years in this career* that I was planning on leaving my six-figure income and pension was absolutely petrifying.

When I woke up on that particular Thursday morning, the first thing I saw was my friend Danielle's morning post on Instagram. It said, "Don't put off until tomorrow the things that are weighing you down today."

It couldn't have been more clear. I needed to quit my job **today**. So, I called my boss during lunchtime and told her that it was time for me to move on. She asked me if I was moving on to work somewhere else or just to focus on my business. I was *so* proud to tell her that I was leaving to be more effective in my own company. The weight was off my shoulders, at least for the night.

A day passed, and I got to gloat to all my coworkers that I was out of there! It felt great, but I knew it was risky to leave my job this time of year. It was almost June and for music school businesses like mine, that means kids are about to quit taking music lessons for the summer. I thought, "It's all good. I've done a great job marketing for the summer, so we'll be fine." I basked in that glory for about eighteen hours.

The next day I got a phone call. It was my office manager calling to let me know that three of our key staff members had quit. Apparently, the company memo that I sent out about tardiness and absenteeism was enough to push them over the edge. I'd now have to tell 70 of my 500 customers within my music school that their teachers quit, effective immediately. Did I mention that this was a week before their big music recitals? Luckily, the staff who left were the ones whom we had already been thinking of letting go. I buckled down and started looking for new staff, asking current workers if they wanted more shifts. And guess what? They did.

I remember sleeping well that night thinking, "Wow, we handled those problems fast." As soon as I turned over from waking up, I saw my daily sales numbers pop up on my phone's email app. It was my office manager again, but this time it was with much worse news. Clients had been calling in to tell us that they wouldn't be continuing for summer enrollment. They were quitting our music lessons. Fifty accounts went out the window just that fast. Each of them represented eighty-three dollars that were supposed to go to me. That meant more than $4,000 of my monthly income would now be gone. This could be a huge problem since I had only allocated myself a $5,000 monthly salary at that point.

Back to square one.

Screw the Business Plan

I figured that the best thing to do to fix this problem was to market my brains out, so I logged onto my dear friend, Facebook. You see, a lot of people mention having problems with Facebook and their security, but Facebook gets me excited. I mean *real* excited. I make more than $90,000 a year just from Facebook.

So, I opened my business page, but something looked weird. Facebook said that I could post something to the business page, but it didn't say that I could post something to *my* page. "Wait up a minute," I thought. "This couldn't be happening."

There it was. My reality. Somehow Facebook had unlinked my role as the "Business Page Owner," and I no longer had access to my Facebook page. Over five years of building, almost 5,000 quality followers on our page, and more than $25,000 spent marketing on Facebook, and the best response they could give me when I inquired via their forum was that Facebook is not in a position to dispute admin roles, and I should either reach out to the original page owner or start a new page if I was the original owner. WHAT?! I'm losing my ability to market on our goldmine that I spent years developing? This couldn't get any worse . . . that was until Sunday morning.

My business is open seven days a week, but I frequently forget that they are even there working because my staff operates without me. On this particular Sunday afternoon around 12:15 p.m., I got a phone call from the receptionist working. She said, "Something happened with Charlese, let me put her on the phone with you." Charlese was one of our newest and most dynamic teachers. The students absolutely loved her. It just so happened that she is also African-American. In business, money is always green but sometimes people only see brown when they look at certain people.

Sobbing through her words, Charlese informed me that as she walked out to her car during her lunch break, the residential neighbor behind our commercial location began calling her an "animal" and other names. He then pointed to her car, and there it was. Dog and cat feces smeared all over her windshield and the handle of her car.

I couldn't help but to hold back tears. Truth be told, I have always had a pit in my stomach when thinking about hiring people of the same racial background as myself because I heard rumors about people in the neighborhood being a bit racist. Regardless, I had never seen this so blatantly displayed at my business in the past five years. "How did I drop the ball in protecting my staff?" I thought. I sat there bewildered, trying to find the words to comfort someone for something that I never had to comfort anybody before.

This all took place within the first seven days after I told my job I was leaving. I only had one week left to work for my boss. The old me who was on the fence for a long time about working for myself would have probably asked my boss to rescind my request to leave and beg to keep my position. The entrepreneurial me knew that these were just hurdles, setbacks. The me that was about to be responsible for her own success or failure knew that I had to be resourceful to solve all these problems, to use the legal knowledge of those who help my company be successful, and the grit to use every moment to make more money since having money makes it much easier to solve problems in your business.

Think about it . . .

Three great employees leave? It's easier to market for their replacements if you have money.

Fifty customers leave? It's easier to market for *their* replacements if you have money.

If Facebook or any of your marketing strategies stop working in your favor? It's easier to continue getting customers if you have money for marketing, using several different methods of advertisement, not just being at the mercy of one. By the way, Facebook quickly resolved our issue. Told you that I loved Facebook!

Employees threatened while at your business location? Well, you sure need money for great surveillance and top-of-the-line attorneys.

    I often tell my staff to take a moment to reflect and be empathetic to the situation at hand, and then to run off like wild maniacs getting more customers to fix the problems we can't fix ourselves. Some people can't handle that. They can't or don't want to handle the problems that owning a business comes with, so they prefer to leave it to their own boss at a traditional job.

    If that's you, that's okay, too. But if you have an ache in your stomach that lets you know you can do this, and you're ready to work . . . then it's time to learn the skills and mind-set that you'll need to turn your profits on and up.

Dictionary.com: money grubber

A person who is aggressively engaged in or preoccupied with making or saving money.

Chapter 2
MONEY GRUBBER

Growing up, we were taught that wanting a lot of money was wrong. It was greed. At some point, our Sunday school teachers and family members alike let us know that money was the root of all evil. Growing up in a typical middle-class family, parents get up every day, went to work, deposited their paychecks, took care of their families, and it was sufficient. Your little sister got that new doll that she begged for and your older brother always seemed to convince your parents to buy him the necessary sporting equipment. Living that routine every day will program you to believe that you only need enough money to pay your bills and the rest was to save up for a rainy day. Every once in a while, you'd want to splurge on something nice, but I learned young that having a superfluous amount of money was only for wealthy people.

It wasn't until adulthood that I realized I hadn't been on any vacations. Our yearly trips were always to visit relatives because our family members lived so spread out. As a kid, you think *this* is vacation. You get to go see your favorite cousins, and it sounds like a lot of fun. This dreamy idea about vacations in Shubuta, Mississippi (my family's hometown) all come crushing down once you realize that your neighbors went on what they considered to be *real* vacations to places like Disney World and Jamaica. Suddenly, you begin to yearn for those over-the-top African safari trips and to swim in the most beautiful bodies of water in the world.

I realized that I was replicating the patterns of all the adults in my life. I woke up every morning, went to my teaching job, worked hard, and got my paycheck to pay my bills. Usually, the money was barely enough. Certainly, I wasn't making enough to stop thinking about upcoming bills or whether or not the wrong check going through could bounce.

I successfully ran my music business for five years while still working at my day job, full time, running myself ragged for no reason. It wasn't until I started taking trips to business conferences that I realized that I wasn't setting up my life to attract money and enjoy the money I'd made. You see, the conferences were all fantastic. Lavish dinners, illuminations, and access to some of the top moneymakers around the country. Just about everyone was making more money than me, and I was *oh so glad* to be in the room with them. But the truth came on the last day of every conference. While I was packing up to race off and catch my flight to get back in time to my day job the next day, everyone else had planned to stay at the conference location for several additional days to *take in what they'd learned,* figure out how to apply it in their businesses, and to enjoy the geographical location that we were visiting.

Basically, I'm racing home to work, and these people are enjoying extended vacations that they get to write off on their taxes!

Once I realized what was happening, I thought that I'd try this strategy for myself. I had planned a trip to Mexico, but it conflicted with conference calls that I was supposed to be on. So, I attended these conferences via Facetime (thanks, Apple), and I worked my ass off from the comfort of my gorgeous hotel room in Riviera Maya at the Hard Rock Hotel.

It was beautiful lying on a hammock as I watched lizards running by at the same time as I was cashing checks. I thought, "This is it!" Realizing that I could be in a bathing suit while earning my money was enough to tell me that I didn't need to be rushing back to my day job. I had seen too much, yet it was just enough to show me that money isn't evil. It's important. We need it for our health. Not just good healthcare, but for us to have peace of mind. Hell! We already know that lacking money is a leading reason for divorce.

We only have but so many years on this earth. If you have an entrepreneurial spirit, you're always going to have the desire to learn what the "next step" is or how to bring in more money. The only answer to this is to enjoy every moment by setting up your lifestyle the way that you want. And you can't do that being broke!

When you're the one person in your family who can't afford vacations, can't send gifts during the holidays, and can't afford to pay for repairs in your home, you realize that money isn't so evil after all. It's a necessity. It's something I love. Something I want to teach my children to love, and most of all, something I want to teach them to understand.

The Money Relationship

Loving and understanding money is like falling in love with your partner. You've got to learn how to attract money, to understand how it works, and what keeps it around so you can keep it. If you don't care about money, you're going to be wasteful and not controlling with it. I'm very much a money grubber. I don't want to leave any money left out there. If I spend money on marketing, I want to know it's gonna bring me customers who will then turn around and bring me more customers, and that those customers will bring me even more customers. I want all of it!

Even though I have many competitors in my area, I'll fight for every single client who will pay me because I want it all! And that's how we must think. Believe me, the guy down the block wants your customers, too. However, I know that what my company has to offer is superior because of the people who provide it, so it's my duty to dominate just like it's your responsibility to do the same. Money and success are not just desirable but they are absolutely vital. They're not the root of all evil but instead the foundation for freedom, choices, and the ability to make a significant impact in this world.

Money and success provide the resources and opportunities to support your family, contribute to causes you believe in, and leave a legacy that will be remembered long after you're gone. Knowing how important money is and the significant role it plays in our lives, many people struggle to truly understand it.

Due in part to the lack of financial education and the societal taboos surrounding money, we don't have transparent conversations about money. People consider money to be just as important as beauty and love because we all want more of each of them, yet money's the one thing that people can't quite figure out how to attract. If you're looking for better beauty you might go get a new hairstyle, new clothes, or even go to extremes such as getting plastic surgery. To find more love, you might try to change your appearance and put yourself in environments where there are more single people looking for a mate. But money is not so easily deceived by appearances and "faking it until you make it." Money requires its respect and doesn't race to people who won't acknowledge and truly believe that money is overflowing around them.

Growing up in a nice suburban neighborhood, I never wanted for very much. My parents always provided what we needed, and we felt pride knowing that we lived in a beautiful home. It wasn't until I left my parent's home as a teenage mother that I learned what it was like to not only need money but to be downright desperate for cash. With a young son to feed, I worked twelve-hour shifts in hopes of making as much money as I could to pay the rent on my mouse-infested apartment in one of the worst neighborhoods of New York. As much as I worked for money, the money never worked for me—and as a result, there was never enough. It wasn't until years later that I realized through my now-flourishing company just how much money was actually out there.

Money Is Everywhere

Since being in business, I've realized that there is money everywhere that you look. In our younger years, our elders taught us that "money was hard to come by, it doesn't fall off of trees, you've got to hold on to the money that you've got and not be too risky with it because there isn't much of it." That was pretty much bull crap, but they said it because they wanted us to understand that THEY couldn't pull money out of nowhere, and that *you* would need to have money somewhere as a backup. I want you to change the way you think and try to undo everything that you've heard.

You *can* pull money out of thin air if you are smart and resourceful.

The Mastery of Money Reappearance

A few Aprils back, I went to a great conference in Ohio that was hosted by my business coach. The guest speaker was the incredible Dan Kennedy. Dan gave us a wealth of information, made us think outside the boxes about our businesses, and then went in for the kill. At the end of his day with us, he was prepared to sell us one of his products. It cost a little more than $3,000. He let everyone know that there was only a limited amount of these products that would be offered that day so that we felt the scarcity. Many of us jumped up to buy and felt grateful for a spot. About an hour later, my business coach wrapped up our day with a final offer for one of *his* services. I *knew* for certain it would be worth it, so I jumped at the opportunity.

There I was, sitting there as the conference ended thinking about the peanut butter and jelly sandwiches that my family would be eating for the remainder of the Spring. Nonetheless, I was amazed. These guys literally just walked into this room, gave us a great experience, and then set up their own future paychecks.

Money Grubbers know how to quickly create products, services, promotions, or other ideas that can get you money when it's not only needed, but when you want it. Things were great once I left that conference until about a month later when my school teaching job informed me, without much notice, that someone else would be working the summer hours that I'd worked for almost ten years. Apparently, they weren't so excited to rehire me for the summer knowing that I'd once again be needing days off to travel. My heart sunk but the entrepreneur in me knew that I had a following of customers who I could convince to pay for my summer bills.

My life changed the year that I learned that I didn't need to pay for anything ever again, and it all started that summer. The idea sounds crazy, but it makes perfect sense. Why are there so many successful people who seem to have everything in the world and then there are those who are always scraping by? It's because those who are always just scraping by only have access to their bank accounts. Successful entrepreneurs have access to the bank accounts of their *followers*.

Did I go and ask my followers to foot the bill for me? No. I created an event for my VIP clients to participate in. It was a performance at Carnegie Hall, and I knew that my top clients would want their little angels to have the opportunity to participate even if for no other reason than to tell their friends that their children performed at Carnegie Hall. I ran a sale for the event, and it sold out in days. Then I set up future income for the event by prepping my clients to purchase tickets. In addition to this event, I set up a promotion giving my clients ten percent off for paying for the year in advance. That promotion alone brought in almost $20,000 in a week without me having to do anything other than send out an email. Needless to say, I had more fun that summer traveling than any year ever!

The realization as an entrepreneur that **my job is to get my followers to pay for my lifestyle** came from Dan Kennedy. If you have not read his book *No B.S. Wealth Attraction in the New Economy* or invested in his Renegade Millionaire System, I highly suggest that you do both immediately.

Rake It Up

Instead of depending on a single paycheck, the money grubbers who acquire the majority of the wealth are creating many ways to get checks coming in. Meanwhile, the average person doesn't want to be bothered finding better ways to make money, or they assert that it's simply unattainable. Listen, you can have one business that has become wildly successful, but the ones who truly enjoy the flow of money are cashing checks while they sleep through *many different* methods. In addition to your business or idea, pick the passive income of your pleasure. Or even pick three!

Dividend income
High yield savings accounts
Real estate
Book sales
Peer-to-peer lending
Become a private lender
Affiliate marketing
YouTube videos
Online store
Create an online course

Create a blog
Vending machine business
Rent out items you already have

There are an enormous amount of methods to bring in money outside of your traditional business. Choose an avenue that you haven't tried yet, and then try another, and repeat.

Wealth Isn't Just for Lucky People

There are many more millionaires and billionaires than we know of. Many of them sit quietly behind the scenes simply enjoying their lives whether at home or in beautiful places abroad. If you check out the *Forbes List* of the wealthiest people, you'll see that there aren't too many new people added to that list as time goes on because the wealthy know how to soak up the money that others refuse to collect. According to the Oxfam Charity, 82% of global wealth generated in 2017 went to the wealthiest 1%. Let's break that down. First, remember that wealth is created and it doesn't generally just appear. Good decisions and actions have to be made along the way and in 2017, more than eighty percent of money went to the top 1%. This is because this small percentage of people understand how to compound returns on their investments and having wealth provides more opportunities to generate even more wealth. The great thing is that it's not too late to begin creating your first round of wealth. It has to begin somewhere and you're just the right person to begin it for your family.

Money Comes to Money

My mom would always say, "Always keep some money in the kitty because money comes to money." I still don't understand the poor kitty concept, but I did understand what she meant about money flowing to money. I mean, it just so happened that I never had money when crises rose up, but every time that I had money in the bank, everything was smooth sailing. Hmph! There must be something to it. And sure enough, there is. You see, money doesn't respond to panic or crisis. It does respond, however, to the belief that there are large sums of money available to meet beyond all your needs, and to the action put in to keep it flowing. Meaning you can't sit on your butt and say, "I believe money will come into my bank account, I BELIEVE money will come to my bank account!" This isn't hocus pocus or a wish upon a star.

Plain and simple: the more money that you make, the more that you will have to spend on marketing and investing. The more money-grubbing skills you acquire, the more resourceful you'll be in making even larger sums of money.

The concept of money coming to money works in many areas of life. Mentoring young college grads, I would hear of them passing up job offers because they believed that better job offers would come along. I would scream, "NO" to the rooftops. Not only can you acquire something easier when you don't need it, but people desire you even more when they see you are wanted elsewhere. A company will be much more likely to hire you if they know their competitor also wants you.

Abundance and Desire Work Hand in Hand

My significant other use to say, "No man wants a woman that no other man wants." It makes sense. I wouldn't want the old, ugly, grumpy guy whom no other woman wants to be with! So, you've got to find a way to keep money flowing into your account through various methods and most of all, managing your money well because it needs to be cared for like a toddler who just found out how to use his legs.

Unsupervised Money Will Run Off Without You

Money is something that must be managed, and you will never meet someone wealthy who does not have a good accountant or someone to supervise where every cent goes. If you're like me, you may hate monitoring your money. The mere idea of opening your online banking may make you nauseous because it feels better not knowing what's happening in there. This fear can stem from previous negative experiences, financial challenges, or the stress associated with managing personal finances. However, it's time to overcome this fear and monitor important data like your bank activity daily. Not only can you catch unauthorized transactions, but it will allow you to understand your spending patterns better and bring you from thinking with scarcity to abundance.

Right now, think about the first few things that you do each day. We all have a routine. Mine is to wake up, wake up the kids, shower, go to Dunkin' for my cup of coffee, drive to the office, and enjoy my cup of joe while sitting at my desk and handling the most important items of the day. How is the first hour of your morning spent?

Within that first hour when you wake up, you've got to check your bank account. Pay attention not just to the balance, but also look at the items that have been deducted from your account. Check to see if they are correct. Now pay attention to the money that you have in your account. This is the money that should be protected, invested, guarded with your life, and most of all, freed to go bring back even more money. The next part of your morning should be spent doing at least one item that will bring you money, including planning how the money you actually have can be used to either market your business, be invested in another business to generate even higher income, or fund projects that will bring you an increased future profit. Don't wait until the money is needed. Unexpected items come up all the time. Rising insurance costs, customer chargebacks from people who scam businesses all the time, and things you'd never expect will come up at the worst times. Get your customers in a constant habit of paying you on schedule.

The amount of time some business owners spend trying to collect payments from customers is incredible. It's exhausting just thinking about chasing down people to pay you, only to find out that they don't even have the money just yet and need "one more day." Even worse, the average business owner feels badly asking for the money that they're owed. It's uncomfortable, causes friction while doing business, and takes an insurmountable amount of time away from the things that matter most in the business, which are marketing and future planning.

One of the best things that you can do for your business is to automate your payments. Collect your money first, get paid early, and eliminate the irritating process of calling or mailing clients who have past due balances. There are many companies that provide very economical processing of electronic payments through credit cards and checks. If your client doesn't feel comfortable paying in advance, then I wouldn't feel

Too Much Too Fast

Once you start to accumulate your share of wealth, no matter how small it may be in the beginning, you start enjoying nicer purchases because you realize that *you can*. Years after my days of picking up quarters off the ground of New York City to purchase the cheapest food from the local deli to feed my son, I'd go on to having a career with a six-figure income at the same time as running a business that was getting close to becoming a million-dollar company. I paid little attention to the comings and goings of the cash but felt blessed that I was able to fulfill the ongoing requests of my children for whatever they asked for. Trips, video games, lavish jewelry. We'd never been so reckless. Well, *I* had never been so reckless. That was until tax time.

I had just fired my last accountant for dragging his feet, causing me thousands of dollars in late fees and re-filing fees. One Thursday morning, my brand-new accountant gave me a call and told me that he had finished my taxes, and my bill was almost $40,000. What the hell! How was that possible? My bill last year was $3,000, and the government paid me the year before! I've got 400 bucks sitting in my personal bank account, so how could *I* possibly owe the government $40,000? It was then that my accountant told me that I had made not only a six-figure income from my day job but that I had squandered an additional $92,000 from my business. I had nothing to

comfortable in their ability to pay you after the fact. For many businesses, this is a nonnegotiable. Remember, get paid first and get paid early.

show for it except a few nice designer bags and pictures from a few lavish vacations in the Caribbean.

Ever since that day, my accountant looks over how I spend our money at the end of each month. If there is something out of the ordinary, he brings it to my attention so that I realize what was spent. Not only do I review my bank account and spending, but I have a highly recommended professional to make sure that my spending is not only practical and legal, but that I'm not going to end up back picking up coins off the streets of Queens, New York, anymore.

"No one has ever become poor by giving."
-Anne Frank

The Power of Giving

When it comes to creating wealth and wealth attraction, there is no greater person that comes to mind than Dan Kennedy. While his principles and philosophies have helped many people establish millionaire incomes, his 90-Day Experiment is directly, if not solely, responsible for my ability to find money where it did not exist and my ability to leave my day job—on my own terms.

The 90-Day Experiment

"Most people focus only on increasing income. But the wealthy are just as concerned or more concerned with increasing equity. So, here's the 90-Day Experiment: Immediately establish a new bank account and call it your Wealth Account. It can be checking, interest-bearing checking, money market.

At first, it doesn't matter. Next, determine a fixed percentage of every dollar that comes your way that will be diverted into that Wealth Account. Something between one and ten percent. You may think you can't do this—"Hey, I can't pay my bills now with one hundred percent of every buck, how will I pay them with ninety percent? Well, maybe you won't. But you aren't now either! So just do it. Pick a percentage, deposit the money, and then do NOT touch it, no matter what. Daily if need be.

You could be poor, getting paid ten dollars a day, decide on one percent, and be putting only ten cents a day into a piggy bank, and even though you would directly accumulate little in ninety days, so many other things would change in your life, you'd still be amazed."

-Dan S. Kennedy,
Author, No B.S. Wealth Attraction in the New Economy

Having a wealth account is not just important, it is an absolute necessity for anyone seeking financial prosperity and freedom. It is the foundation upon which your financial empire is built. A wealth account is not merely a bank account with numbers on a statement; it is a mindset, a commitment to accumulating and growing wealth. It is about consistently and relentlessly putting money aside, treating it as a valuable resource that can be strategically deployed to seize opportunities and create exponential returns.

A wealth account can be the vehicle that allows you to take control of your financial destiny, escape the shackles of mediocrity, and begin your path of limitless abundance. Without a dedicated wealth account, you are merely drifting aimlessly in the sea of financial uncertainty, missing out on the incredible opportunities that await those who are wise enough to invest in their own financial future. You invest in others all the time when you go into any store. It's time that you invest in the one you're stuck with- yourself.

Chapter 3
THE MASTER OF MARKETING WINS

If you're like most new business owners, you're devoting your time to cracking the code on finding customers. We all know our own crafts and can be great with people, but all this means nothing because the struggle of getting customers is very real.

Your business may be the type that gets paid when customers make one-time purchases, you charge monthly like a subscription service, or even when you're done completing a project for them. But there comes a time for most new entrepreneurs when they can't seem to break their current point of sales. That's because there's only so far you can go without marketing. Not just any marketing, but the insane marketing that reaches everyone who might be willing to pay you a dollar.

Your #1 role in your company is to be a master of marketing. In the words the great Grant Cardone, "Promote, promote, promote."

The business that I happen to be in has memberships and allows me to bill my customers monthly. Once we hit the one-year mark, I was frustrated that I couldn't seem to break the one hundred-customer per/month mark. We had about ninety-three monthly customers, and a quarter of them were coming damn near for free. I was giving the whole kitchen away! That was when I started Googling, "How to find customers." Seriously, I became *that* desperate, but that's how desperate you've got to become to find the piece that you're missing to finding more customers. After joining a network of marketers, I quickly went from fifty *paid* clients being billed monthly to billing more than 500 clients each month. This can only happen when each day is devoted to mastering the art of marketing. After all, it is my number one priority to bring in customers. You've got to adopt this new job title as a priority starting today, putting it before anything else.

If you're one of the lucky people with a marketing staff—great job! You *still* need to be promoting your butt off and making sure that no stone is left unturned in filling your money pipeline. It feels great once you learn how to delegate important tasks to others within your company and it's necessary for you to delegate, but you can't ever turn over the wheel completely for something as crucial as your marketing. It is the heartbeat of your company. Once it stops beating, every other function stops. They'll be no sales team, no finance team, no customer service team. Nothing. Marketing is senior to everything else so it needs to be the top concern for entrepreneurs.

For the average small business owner without a marketing team, the idea of being a master of marketing can sound overwhelming. Beyond the fliers, telling the people at church about your business, and giving out your latest business cards, it can be hard learning how to market a company. Nonetheless, it is the one thing that is nonnegotiable. You must market in dozens of different ways every single month. And I would suggest you try much more. The worst thing you can do is go out and give the fancy guys from the marketing company you found online all your money. Based on the biblical story of Noah's Ark, people have thrown around the phrase, "If you build it, they'll come!"

Those people lied their asses off.

No one outside of your small network is coming simply because they don't know about you. Your primary concern each day must be to be at the front of your customer's mind. If you're someone who is on a budget, you can obviously start small by creating fliers, putting out lawn signs around the community, and getting current customers to refer their friends. However, you're going to need a solid marketing budget.

The Economical Entrepreneur

The image of the old business owner hoarding his money so that no one can take it away is as vivid as can be in my mind. With everyone trying to take our money away, it's no wonder that we're petrified to spend money. Still, not advertising is not an option. It will never be an option. In the words of Thomas Jefferson, "The man who stops advertising to save money is like the man who stops the clock to save time". It will never work. Stopping a clock doesn't create more time and avoiding the action of spending money to promote your company won't lead to savings in the long run. Advertising your product or service is the most vital component of any successful business operation. In fact, most companies who fail early are ones who simply didn't have the skills or money to get their company known. Failing to advertise may have temporary savings but will not secure brand recognition and will decrease both your sales and future opportunities.

You simply can't make money without spending money. Resourceful people will find a way to rub two nickels together and get a dollar. Creativity and resourcefulness will get you far, but there are simply some paths to collecting payments that require cash up front. I didn't understand this until a mentor of mine told me to start keeping lines of credit available. I told him that I missed being debt free and wished I could go back to not having any business debt. He reminded me that small business budgets need small lifelines and bigger business budgets require bigger access to cash. This same thing holds true about investing in marketing. Cut corners on staffing, cut corners on new equipment or furniture, but never cut corners on your marketing.

Walking Billboard

Marketing covers everything from advertising and promotions to sales and more. But before you prep any of your outside marketing, you've got to mold your walking billboard—you. You should, today and forever, be the most vocal, articulate, and persuasive person about your business. Beginning as soon as you walk in the room, people should wonder what your business is and leave the room knowing exactly what you've got to offer.

One of the biggest issues that I had for the first few years of owning a business was feeling too ashamed of telling people that I owned a company. I'm not sure if it was because I was shy about it, undeserving, or that people would judge me. Still to this day, I'm not sure what the reason was. However, I always got the very uncomfortable dumb questions that would soon come along like, "Did you always want to do this?" "How many clients do you have?" and a slew of other questions that always seemed to make me second-guess myself for no real reason. What I didn't realize is that I was cutting myself off to dozens and dozens of customers who would buy from me because they already trusted me and had faith in me simply from knowing who I was. Once I realized that the people I was spending my time around were buying from my company and spending quite a great deal, I realized that I had to be a walking billboard for my company.

It's not all about appearances, but the first thing you want to determine is what type of appearance you want to keep. Do you want to present yourself as well-groomed, clean-cut, with the freshly pressed shirt, or are you at the point in your life where your business doesn't rely on you being a representative for it in public so you can wear anything that you want? Whatever stage you're in, you want people to see trust, integrity, and innovation every time that they're in your presence. Most of all, they should always hear from you the latest news of what's going on in your business. Start today by developing a simple elevator pitch.

Having an elevator pitch is one of the easiest and most important ways to get your idea out there when meeting someone. This should be a concise, compelling, and well-crafted summary your business idea. According to Seth Godin, your elevator pitch should be "so compelling that the person you're with wants to hear more even after the elevator ride is over." If done right, your pitch will effectively communicate the unique value proposition of your product or service, the benefits, and how someone can continue to be involved with you as a customer, referrer, or investor. Be confidant, professional, and make sure you leave a lasting impression.

For years, I never considered the need to create an elevator pitch. It's hard enough for me to explain to myself the purpose of my business on some days when I feel like the train has run over me! But this elevator pitch is often what keeps business owners off the unemployment line. If you ask anyone who's been on *Shark Tank* or anyone who ever had to pitch their idea to an investor, they'll tell you that their elevator pitch saved their life. Today, take five minutes to sit down and write a few sentences about the mission and purpose of your business. Write down what problem you're solving, who it's for, and what your upcoming plans are in the company. Even if you've done this before, take five minutes to update your phrases or even phrasing. The right words matter to those who want to write a check to you.

Marketing to the Right People

There aren't too many things that are worse than never marketing, but a close second would be marketing to the completely wrong crowd. Most of us aren't billionaires, so where we put our marketing money matters a lot. Throwing it to the wind is useless. As the owner of a children's business, I've learned that I can't market to granddads and only sometimes to grandmothers. They aren't the ones buying from me. Take the time to figure out exactly who your customers are and target your advertisements in their direction.

When it comes to targeting your clients, Facebook is really on to something. It's actually a bit more than just their ability to creep out its users by making them wonder how Facebook knows everything about them. Facebook and other social media platforms have become masters of encouraging users to provide optional information about themselves, such as their marital status, profession, and even political views. Facebook couldn't have been any smarter because they connect businesses like mine with the consumer who has a need to fill. An example of this is on my Facebook account where I'm connected to many weight loss groups. See, when I started this mission of losing a hundred pounds, I needed tips from others online. But sure enough, the advertisements that I see on my timeline are not for Starbucks, they are for Burger King. Yes, freaking Burger King. They market to the inner fat girl in me, and I get to sit at the computer drooling even though I know that I need a Whopper like I need a hole in the head. Nonetheless, Burger King knew not only what person to target, but also where to find me.

Burger King isn't going to market on the Disney Channel very frequently because the kids aren't the ones doing the food shopping after a long day of work. Similarly, spending money on newspaper ads rarely is of use to me, because most parents in my area aren't looking at the newspaper, they're online. So, my marketing must not only include online advertisements, but I've got to be able to find these future customers online.

Take a moment and write out who your prospective customers are. Now write out the places these people usually frequent, channels they watch on television, radio stations that they tune into, and print material that they read. Now that you'll know where to find them, be sure you direct your message to them.

Tracking

One of the most important aspects of marketing that new entrepreneurs often miss are the details about how their customers heard about them. If you ask most new business owners how many new customers they got this year and where those customers came from, they'll either say that they have no clue or lie and say, "Mostly word of mouth." Truth of the matter is that most people don't like to pay attention to where their sales come from. But if you don't, how are you supposed to know which of your marketing dollars are being well-spent versus the ad campaign that you should never run again?

Tracking where your customers are coming from has to be a part of your sales process. When someone inquires about your business, you have to ask them how they heard about your company. Even if they're inquiring online, you need a section that asks them to let you know where they heard about you. When a customer purchases something from you, same thing—you've got to find out where they heard about you. Lastly but most importantly, schedule a day each month when you review where your customers are coming from. Find out what's working and what's not. If an area of your marketing is not bringing you the customers that it should, change it up to see the next month if it's worth keeping.

Stay in control of how your business is being displayed to the public and don't be afraid to try out new ideas. The only person who doesn't get to eat well at the end of the day is the timid marketer who pays no attention to the facts within the business and acquiring the next customer.

The Power of Referrals

There is nothing more valuable to a company than its customers. Referrals have a way of changing a business into an overnight success because everyone wants the next best thing. Your customers are the ones who are going to tell their friends and families what that next best thing will be, so it's important that they think of your name whenever they think of the product or service that you offer. Get your family using the service and ask them to send people your way so that you'll be on the top of their mind when the opportunity arises. Mark Zuckerberg from Facebook said, "People influence people. Nothing influences people more than a recommendation from a trusted friend. A trusted referral influences people more than the best broadcast message. A trusted referral is the Holy Grail of advertising." This is because people have a significant impact on one another and tend to value the opinions of others more than they do impersonal messages or advertisements.

When a recommendation comes from someone we trust, it holds more weight and is more likely to sway our decisions.

As the person who cuts the checks in my business, what I say holds no water compared to a friend. Family members and friends are quick to share businesses that fix their problems or offer exceptional customer service because they want their friends to know that they found it first.

Some people struggle to ask for referrals, but this can be the easiest way to grow if you do it right. First of all, you must provide exceptional service or products to be worth referring. When you have successfully met the needs of your customer, politely ask if they know anyone else who might benefit from what you offer. You can do this in your newsletters, emails, social media posts, or any other channel of communication. Then, create a culture of referrals by offering great incentives for people to refer friends such as discounts, rewards, or anything else that would benefit your customer. Don't forget to get online reviews and testimonials from your customers as they serve as a powerful insight for prospective customers. Most importantly, show gratitude to those who refer friends. A heartfelt thank you or acknowledgment goes a long way in developing longtime relationships with your customers.

In the last three years, my customers have referred more than 300 friends. Each new customer is worth $2,352 to me. Since I have a subscription business, those 300 customers add more than $700K to my business each year. Promote referrals. Ask for referrals.

Shopping Like Your Mother

If you're a parent in any capacity, you know what it's like to shop around. Think back to the days when your mother would shop for your back-to-school clothes and supplies. It must've felt like everything cost a gazillion dollars and mom was willing to take the best deal that she could get. Times may have changed, but everyone secretly wants to be like your mother and get the good deal.

An important aspect of marketing is getting the right offer to new clients. It doesn't matter what it is. Buy one-get one free, take ten percent off, or almost anything. But people want to know that they have the option to get the deal. Find a way to let them know it's for a limited time and choose an expiration date that's going to get them through your door quickly.

A lot of entrepreneurs don't feel like they should provide a discounted offer to get customers in the door. Half of your prospective customers won't care a bit about having a deal but to the other half, it's a very big deal.

Major League Marketing

If you want to be king of the land, you have to claim all the property. That means having your company name everywhere. Once your potential clients see it several times, they're going to know that you're the big guy (or gal) in town. They'll come to you because they'll assume that everyone else uses your company. Some of the cheaper methods of marketing include free posting on websites like Craigslist, email marketing, sending out newsletters, asking for referrals, creating a blog, or investing in every marketing item that Vistaprint has online (using the online promo codes, of course). But the real big boy marketers can reach the masses through Google advertising, social media, magazines, and so much more! Stack those chips. Make a list of at least twenty ways that you can advertise, assign each item a budget, and test them all out. Remember, this is your number one job.

Negative Feelings Toward Marketing

Although I've already told you the story of my first year in business, I didn't tell you about my feelings about marketing. First of all, I had no clue what it really meant to market. My version included fliers, handing out a few business cards, and calling around to a couple of schools to ask if they'd support my business. I'm actually pretty surprised that no one called the cops, assuming that I was a nut job. What I did know was that I was completely lost and that I didn't like the idea of putting my business name everywhere because I was afraid of people negatively comparing my business to the next local superstar company. For that reason, my sales flat lined.

Dan Kennedy once said that "if you have emotional hang-ups about sales and marketing, don't 'like' it, are convinced you aren't good at it, and refuse to hunker down and get good at it, I just don't have much hope for you when it comes to wealth attraction." This is because sales and marketing are at the core of generating income and entrepreneurs must make sales and marketing a priority. These vital functions are the driving force for business growth. Without effective sales strategies and marketing initiatives, even the most innovative and exceptional products or services will fail to be successful.

Sales and marketing help entrepreneurs stay competitive in their industry by creating brand awareness, building a strong customer base, and standing out among competitors.

So many people simply hate marketing just as much as they hate accounting. The great news is that marketing is something that can be learned. Once you find out what helps you to acquire customers, you've got to make this practice a routine. If nothing else gets done each day, time should be spent trying to acquire a new customer. You can't have negative feelings toward the process of making money.

Chapter 4
PAY YOURSELF FIRST

Some entrepreneurs grab money from their savings accounts or some other financial windfalls to start up and begin operating their businesses. These people, like me, don't take a paycheck until we realize that we should've been paying ourselves all along. The other type of entrepreneur is the one who jumps into business because they're broke and needs to start collecting money as soon as possible. Those people wisely figure out whatever they need to do to collect a profit before anything else.

" 86.3% of small business owners said they take a yearly salary of less than $100k. 30.07% of small business owners don't take a salary."

-Fundera.com

Not only is paying yourself extremely important to your own personal success and sanity, but you've got to make paying yourself *first* a top priority.

You may be thinking, "How in the world can I afford to pay myself first when I can barely pay for business rent, utilities, or even my staff?" You can! But it starts with changing your mind-set away from the Sales − Expenses = Profit model that many business owners follow. Author and entrepreneur Mike Michalowicz presented the concept of taking profit first to bewildered business owners, and they've been raking in the cash ever since they realized that their expenses must be planned out based on what's left over *after* profit is taken. Check it out.

TRADITIONAL ACCOUNTING IS KILLING YOUR BUSINESS

"Since the dawn of time—or shortly thereafter—businesses have kept track of their earnings and expenditures using essentially the same method:

Sales – **Profit** = Expenses

If you manage the numbers like most entrepreneurs, you start with sales (the top line) and then subtract costs directly related to the delivery of your offering (product or service). Then you subtract all the other costs you incur to run your business: rent, utilities, employee salaries, office supplies, and other administrative expenses, sales commissions, taking your client out to lunch, signage, insurance, etc., etc. Then you pay taxes. Then, and only then, do you take your owner's distribution (owner's salary, profit distribution, etc.).

Let's be honest, entrepreneurs hardly ever take anything close to a real salary, and good luck telling the government that you decided to skip taxes this year so that you could pay yourself. Finally, after all that, you post your company's profit. And if your experience is like the majority of entrepreneurs, you never get to 'finally.' When you're waiting for the leftovers, at best you'll get scraps."

-Mike Michalowicz

The process of paying yourself first can seem absolutely ridiculous to the business owner who is simply trying to have enough money to make payroll each month or keep the electric account up to date. But you've got to ask yourself right out of the gate when you start or right at this moment if you've already been in business, "how is any of this hard work worth it if you can't pay yourself?" The goal of getting into business wasn't to starve, and it wasn't to pay everyone else's bills. Not only do you deserve a piece of the pie, but you're the one working the most and with everything to lose. So, I'd say that you deserve the biggest piece of the pie.

Mike Michalowicz details in his Profit First book the many different types of bank accounts that you can open and simply transfer the correct amount in each month. I encourage you to start even simpler. Pick one day per month that you can visit your business budget for the upcoming month. Don't leave anything out. Literally go through your bank accounts to see what money you need to spend monthly to keep your business afloat. Based on that budget, see if there are areas that you're spending in that you don't need. Then cut them off immediately.

Next, determine how much would be left over for you after paying all of these expenses and putting some money into your business savings account. If it's not what you need, then you'll need to reevaluate the expenses that you believe you truly need.

What service do you use that you can operate without?
What supplies do you buy that aren't required?
What could you replace with something more cost effective?

Example of Paying Yourself First

BUSINESS NAME	MONTHLY BUDGET
Monthly Sales	65,000
Prepaid Accounts	1,500
TOTAL GROSS	63,500
EXPENSES	40,763
Rent	5,000
Payroll fees	200
Insurances	400
Staff and payroll taxes	20,000
Monthly website fee	13
CC fees	2,000
Utilities (gas/electric/phone)	900
Business memberships	500
Computer software	200
Constant Contact	50
Marketing	4,000
Supplies	800
Savings for taxes and rainy day	4,200
Payment to attorneys	1,000
Payment to accountant	200
Miscellaneous	300
Equipment rental	500
Donations	500
Total Expenses	38,763
Total Profit	22,737

Step 1. Transfer a percentage of profit into your savings.

Step 2. Transfer your accurate profit first before paying others.

Who can be replaced in your business if needed?

Who and what are "untouchable" and necessary?

Paying Yourself Is Nonnegotiable

You wouldn't (and shouldn't) ever expect an employee to work for free, so it's unreasonable to expect that for yourself. The art of paying yourself first simply requires:

1. Knowing how much you can afford to pay yourself
2. Taking your checks or disbursements first and on schedule
3. Staying within your monthly budget

If you can't do that, you may need to have an accountant handle those three areas for you. And there's nothing wrong with that. Some of the best money movers can gracefully get money to leave one person's wallet and come to their own but are terrible at managing their own money. Being good at one thing doesn't make you naturally good at the other. But it does mean that you should get help from professionals to keep you in line if that's something you struggle with.

Hard Times

Paying ourselves first to feed our families and live rewarding lives is important, but we know rainy days will come. There are going to be many occasions when you have no idea where the money will come from for that past due bill, the upcoming order that you need to break even next month, or even your own rent. Trust and believe, you need a backup plan. Where would you get the money?

Consider Your Resources

Make a list of each of your resources that fall into the categories below.

Friends with money who may be interested in giving you a loan with interest

1. _____
2. _____
3. _____

Family with money who may be interested in giving you a loan with interest

1. _____
2. _____
3. _____

Banks or credit unions who might loan you money

1. _____
2. _____
3. _____

Personal or Business line of credit

1. _____
2. _____
3. _____

Nontraditional business loans

 1. _____
 2. _____
 3. _____

Personal or business credit cards

 1. _____
 2. _____
 3. _____

401K or equivalent accounts that hold your money

 1. _____
 2. _____
 3. _____

Saving accounts you can tap in to

 1. _____
 2. _____
 3. _____

Crowd funding possibilities

 1. _____
 2. _____
 3. _____

Angel investor possibilities

1. _____
2. _____
3. _____

Unused equipment you can sell

1. _____
2. _____
3. _____

In hard times, I've had to use almost all of the options listed in the previous pages, but I've found the following rules keep my business on steady ground.

1. Have your savings automatically drafted each month (and hide the account from your online view so you don't think about it).
2. Have your own salary automatically drafted each month or quarter after your business is paid.
3. Borrow from yourself as long as you can (savings, credit cards, 401k, etc.). You'll charge yourself less interest.
4. As your business gets bigger, you'll need more money. Secure a line of credit but don't let them bully you into ridiculous interest rates. They'll want your soul and unborn kids next.

SECTION II
Assembly of the WOW TEAM

Chapter 5
THE POWER OF MENTORSHIP

About a year into business, I realized that there was a huge learning curve in the transition from unprofitable to profitability. The first year of my start-up was spent giving away so much of my business and trying to keep every dollar protected. Although there were several small things that completely changed my business, the one step that initiated all the later improvements was the action of hiring a business coach in my field.

Who would think that people would hire business coaches for more than a pep talk and some inspiration? I was already motivated and didn't need someone giving me a hard time when I was already giving myself a hard time! Nonetheless, I was reaching a desperate time. After twelve months of simply running the business because it was fun, I realized that I didn't want to keep dumping my bi-weekly paychecks from my nine-to-five job to support a lousy company.

I jumped online to search for answers but what I got was a whole bunch of garbage written by dozens of MBAs who never ran a successful company. After a while, I started Googling, *"how to get customers, how to find clients, how to make a sale, how to get MUSIC students,"* and once I asked my dear friend *Google* for a specific request, it gave me my answer. I had no clue that there was an entire organization devoted to helping music school owners or business coaches who focused only on helping entrepreneurs like me get more money. Who knew? Well, the only problem now is that the mentor I found wanted almost $1,500 just to get started with him and another hundred bucks a month every month after that. Did I mention that this was the month before Christmas? More specifically, two paychecks before Christmas? I'm a single mom. If I'm not buying it, it ain't gettin' *bought*.

I sat my boys down and talked to them about what they wanted. Unfortunately, we had to have several real-life discussions about limiting our *wants* to make ends meet. We spoke about the need to be frugal, make tough decisions, and to work out a plan. That same day, I requested to join this business coach's army of music school owners, and within minutes **I was connected to more than one hundred people just like me.** I couldn't believe it! All the questions that I had during the previous 365 days since opening my business were laid right out for me with answers I couldn't believe I hadn't thought of. Did I mention, I hadn't even spoken to the coach yet, and his program had already paid for itself?

It's much easier to pay a coach for the right answers than to spend dozens of unbillable hours setting yourself up for future failure.

Having mentorship and a solid education in your field is not optional.

Have you ever heard about product junkies? You know, those people who follow a bunch a business coaches online who tell you how you're gonna crank out your first million? They tell you how you're worth so much more than your scars and your current situation. Yeah, these people are getting rich, all right. Rich off of you! Instead of selling you actionable marketing systems, they are selling hopes and dreams. I can't cash dreams!

The problem isn't the business coaches who have all these different programs to sell you. The common variable between you and each of the failed attempts to finally get rich from these programs is YOU! You weren't ready or didn't invest with the right person.

Business owners require mentorship and an investment in your business education.

Cutting costs is one of the smartest strategies in a business, unless the money you are spending will lead to future income. Since we're so programmed to cut down our expenses, it's understandable that you'd be hesitant about investing in a mentor or business coach. If you're just starting out, there are websites like www.score.org that can connect you with a free or low-cost mentor. Before I bit the bullet with my business coach, I found a wonderful woman through the Internet who helped me get the basics started such as a website and social media pages. She would encourage me to set things up, and I would holler back at her a few weeks later. The only problem with this is that it slows your pace. When you invest in high level help, it ensures that you act with speed to implement.

Paying for a credible business coach who specifically coaches people in my field allowed me to get details about *how* to set everything up, what needed to be included in my content, and **how to get the sale every time.** I didn't need someone to keep cheering me on, I needed direction.

Invest in Yourself

Since you're the captain steering the way of your business, it's going to be no one else's fault but your own if you crash and burn. If so much rides on your ability to lead, innovate, and grow your company, then it only makes sense for you to invest in yourself so that you learn how to operate the monster that you've created. Spending money on a quality coach is not where you want to skimp.

The initial payment that I paid my business coach was to purchase the marketing program—basically everything that I needed to know about my business *before* I started it. Then he started billing me a hundred bucks a month. Most people can't imagine handing over a hundred bucks to a stranger, let alone paying a business coach almost a thousand dollars. But within the first ninety days of applying what my new mentor was teaching me about my business, our profits tripled.

I didn't think much of it until I went to his conference and met other people in my profession. It was absolutely wild! A room full of people who had the same type of employees as me, the same type of complaints from customers, and so on. One thing I realized as I mingled with the new crowd of future friends was that those with high performing businesses had a higher level of business coaching membership and got more time with my coach. So, I did the natural thing and jumped on the more expensive monthly membership.

By this point, my family really thought I was crazy, but as time went on I noticed that my income had now tripled again. So, after another two years had gone by, my business coach offered an even more selective coaching program that provided his top clients with even more time with him to utilize his expertise. I currently pay more than $1,000 a month for that membership alone, but when I consider this guy taking my business from a $50,000 per year business to a $1 million company, I don't mind paying him a grand each month. It's all relative, and he pays his business coach a ton more than what he charges me. So, understand there are many different levels in the business coaching world. But you do need to find the right coach—one who teaches you how to grow your business, hand over fist, year after year.

Business coaches or even simple mentors aren't meant to make you feel warm and fuzzy. They're not supposed to tell you everything that you wanted to hear. Their purpose is to guide you to practice habits and make decisions that you may not have made prior and to hold you accountable for making progress. One thing not to do is to expect a business coach to be your friend. They can serve as a source for motivation, consulting, advising, or inspiration but they aren't therapists. They're meant to be transparent and to provide strategy in actionable steps. Discussing the past with them is of no use and devalues your time together. To make the most of our time with a coach or mentor, be sure to articulate your goals to your coach so have a clear understanding of what you want to achieve. Secondly, take good notes during coaching sessions as most are brief. If they allow you to record them, then record them so you can refer back to your conversation when you have the same issues in the future. Most importantly, action and accountability are vital for hitting your targets.

A coach doesn't want to work with someone who drags their feet and creates excuses. How are they supposed to get paid if you're not progressing and your pockets aren't getting heavier? You'll eventually be broke, blame it on the coach, and go out of business shortly thereafter or at least stunt your growth like many business owners who are comfortable perpetually spinning in the same income bracket. Be sure to evaluate your progress frequently and celebrate you wins along the day.

Make the Best of Your Coaching Time

Your investment in business coaching can be some of your best-spent dollars or a complete waste of time. Even though 90 percent of the time you can get a great deal of information just by listening to your coach ramble on about business since they have a great deal of information that you can learn from, you'll actually experience growth if you are prepared for your coaching call.

Regardless of the amount of coaching time that you have paid for, plan out a long list of questions that are driving you nuts in your business. Make the list twice as long as you think it should be because many business coaches are fast-paced and can get your questions answered quickly. Once you've made that list, be sure to place your most important questions at the top. My inquiries tend to follow this pattern: (a) a question about my long-term growth, (b) a question about something that's frustrating me that I need a quick solution to, (c) a question about improving my marketing for the current season, and (d) everything else. Know all your business statistics and be ready to take a lot of notes.

Coach as a Lifeline to the Network

Behind every great coach is a group of successful entrepreneurs. Many of them have been in business for decades, and best of all, the ones who have a coach are invested in both learning more and continuing to grow their business. These are the people whom you want to seek out. If you connect enough with them, then your investments in a business coach will be worth more than you'll ever imagine. Each person you meet represents someone to share a great idea with you, a cross-marketing opportunity, advertising knowledge, and a host of other benefits that last as long as you'll keep those connections going.

Chapter 6
BUILD RELATIONSHIPS THAT MATTER

I landed my dream gig fresh out of college. I couldn't believe it! When I came in to meet with my new supervisor and soon-to-be mentor, Anne-Marie, she seemed so excited about the prospect of me working for their organization. It was like she saw something in me that I had no clue even existed. She set me up in my classroom and walked me down a long hallway to introduce me to my colleagues. As we walked, she said, "You're going to love your coworkers. They are some of the finest, most talented individuals you'll ever meet. But listen, when they ask you to go out to lunch, you say yes."

It was one of the oddest things that I'd ever heard, but years later I realized exactly what she meant. My success at that job had nothing to do with my talent and tenacity, but everything to do with the relationships that I took time to develop. Over the years, my colleagues and I created together, built unique programs, and even celebrated personal successes together. Getting to know each other's strengths and even feeding off each other's connections helped us to take our organization to even higher levels. As years passed, we even traveled to other countries together. We grew to trust one another, not just as friends, but even as business partners over time. I was now making money from the relationships I'd formed.

Anne-Marie was right. I did have some of the most innovative and inspiring coworkers ever. And I never, ever said no to lunch.

"Thank You" Goes a Long Way

Not only are great relationships important for friendships and future partnerships, but they are also the lifeline of every company. Companies with poor relationships between employers and employees never survive the rough times. When I think of rough times, the first thing that comes to mind are how my employees handled our survival during the Covid-19 shutdown. My great or even mediocre employees did their best and were appreciative not to be forced into unemployment. However, employees who I did not have a relationship with quickly soured and did everything they could to see the business shut down even if it meant permanently. These are the same type of people who make up most organizations.

Entrepreneurs eat, breathe, and live their company. It's often what we drink cocktails over at night and what we wake up thinking about each morning. Our employees don't wake up in the middle of the night thinking about the payroll checks clearing or the tax bill that needs to get paid. It's not *their* job to worry about all the details of our company, and it's also not their benefit to receive the upcoming profits. Nonetheless, you must have a way to get them to *buy into* your company. Your values. You. They've got to trust you and feel appreciated by you all the time.

There are many ways to show your gratitude toward your staff. Even though it's so easy to show them gestures of thanks, we get too wrapped up in all the current issues going on that appreciation gets lost in translation. To keep the good vibes flowing in my business, I focus on these four core beliefs in maintaining good relationships with my staff:

1. Incentives
2. Bread breaking
3. Verbal thanks
4. Reality checking

First of all, everyone has to have an incentive to work. If they know that they can come to work, do a mediocre job, and get paid the same amount each week, which is usually too small anyway, then they aren't going to want to do an exceptional job for your customers. As an entrepreneur, you want your incentives to your staff to reflect your respect for them and appreciation for all that they do. My incentives reward them with cash bonuses, raises if they meet a certain sales goal, and paid time off so that they can lead a normal, mentally healthy lifestyle.

The next is breaking bread or eating with your staff. Just as Anne-Marie encouraged me to eat with my colleagues, she also provided opportunities for all the staff to sit, and eat together. We talked and learned about one another and took the time to find out about each other's lives. Maybe you don't care about what your employees have going on in their lives, but that information has everything to do with the success of your business. Taking the time to sit and eat together gives you that chance to see each other as human. To hear how life is for the other person and connect simply as human beings. So, go ahead, invite your staff out to dinner to talk about upcoming goals and happenings in the business. If you don't take the temperature of your staff early, you'll never have a heads-up when something is going awry.

The two words everyone secretly wants to hear is "thank you." The difference between a jackass boss and a boss with a crowd who respects them is their ability to thank the employees for everything and to thank them in advance. I may ask my office manager to complete a task, but it generally sounds like this, "Vanessa, please reach out to Mr. Johnson to update his payment for this month. Thank you." Provide directives but provide them with gratitude. It will go a long way.

As entrepreneurs, we're living in this bubble thinking that our staff is immortal, above sickness and theft. They're not. They are regular people just like you and me. Their kids get sick, and they might have to be out of work for a while. They might have an abusive husband and need to move out of their home during your biggest week of business in the year. It never works out in perfect timing, but you've got to remember to give yourself a reality check. These people have problems and aren't going to always be perfect. The difference is that their issues are on display to you.

> **"I speak to everyone in the same way, whether he is the garbage man or the president of the university."**
>
> **– Albert Einstein**

Years ago, I had the pleasure of hearing Colin Powell speak about relationships. He said that he learned so much during his years working in the Pentagon but that the most important thing he figured out was that he needed to treat everyone with the highest level of respect. At the end of each night, he would thank the cleaners and janitorial staff the same way that he would speak to and thank politicians he had encountered. As a result, their productivity remained high and they demonstrated a great deal of pride in the quality of their work.

Imagine that. If we treat people as though the work that they do matters on all scales, then their work will matter to them, and they'll outperform others because it *matters.*

Consider the last person you remember who paid you no mind in a career situation. For me, I recall a math teacher with whom I taught when I was a public school music teacher. This math teacher was very serious about her subject, and this silly thing called music was just getting in the way of her pulling up her student's math scores. As a result, she could walk down a hallway without making eye contact or even saying hello to me, *or anyone else, for that matter*. This continued for almost ten years.

Now even though you're hopefully not a type of person who would do something like that, think about the staff you currently work with or have worked with in the past. Who do you usually speak to at work? Which employees do you lack eye contact or discussion with on a regular basis? These are the people you want to reach out to. *Immediately.* Say hello. Tell them thank you. Now, repeat.

Customer Relationships

If you believe that your customer is just a dollar sign, then you've cut off your hand to future money beyond that transaction. People are leery of spending their money with anyone who they don't know well, so you've got to prove that they should give you their money. Even if you have the best product, service, AND customer service, your customers must buy in to *you* and your company.

Customers want to connect to someone and have a reoccurring place to visit because we're all creatures of habit. No one wants the vulnerability of using new companies all the time. Not to mention, if you provide something great, they want to tell all their friends about you.

Let this be the season that you get to know your customers a little more. Speak to them on a first name basis and require your staff to do so as well. Ask them about their families and upcoming vacations. Get to know what they love and be thoughtful when the opportunity arises. If you see something in the store along the way that you know they'll love, *grab it!* An economical purchase to win over your customer's attention costs a whole lot less than paying to get new customers.

Building Loyalty Through Business

There's a friend of mine who works for a certain network marketing company that ships out products to customers. My friend's goal through this company is to encourage all her friends to purchase these products and to also find others who want to get into the business. I have my own reasons for not wanting to be bothered with some of these companies, but more than anything, I see very little ability to bond with my customers and get their loyalty if someone else is communicating with them, and I have no control in the quality of what they're receiving. I want to build an army of followers who I can get to buy from me over and over, and then run off to invite their friends to buy from me, too.

At a recent conference, I had the pleasure of meeting Hotel Impossible's Anthony Melchiorri and he even paid a visit to my business as he lives here in New York also. When I asked him what the most important aspect of customer service was to help us blow customers away with an incredible experience, he simply stated, "Everything matters." Anthony is right. Every single detail matters. Anthony's hit show Hotel Impossible might be a hit because of his no-nonsense way of communicating how hotels can drastically improve their building and profits, but his true success must be a by-product of his belief that every matters. From the smell in the room, the smile from a receptionist, or the ability to follow up with a customer- every single thing matters. When you follow this approach, you will realize that everything is marketing and by approaching each area in your business this way, you'll win the loyalty of your customers.

Loyalty is developed through someone's faith in your company and your ability to blow them away every single time. I'll talk more about the WOW experience later in another chapter, but when was the last time that you blew your customers away? We're not just talking about showing up to your appointments and sending out their product on time. Maybe it was a time when you went above and beyond acknowledging that you heard their old aunt had been sick. It could also be a company planned event that you went completely *over the top* for. When you show pride in the details and getting to know your customers, they begin to notice. And you'll notice that they stay longer. They spend more money, and they refer their friends.

In my company, every detail matters. The small things and the smallest people. Those who clean our floors and those who only spend ten dollars sitting next to the customer who gives me almost $1,000.

Bad Reputations Ruin Good Relationships

Warren Buffet is well known for expressing how important a good reputation is in business and how you could spend decades building the perfect reputation just to have it ruined by an employee or one poor decision by the owner. One of his best quotes is "lose money for the firm and I will be understanding. Lose a shred of reputation for the firm and I will be ruthless." These are words for every entrepreneur to live, eat, breathe, and die for. Employees make mistakes all the time. In fact, you'll learn that they'll make decisions that cost the company routinely when you take your eyes off them even if it's by mistake and I'm okay with that. I'll always do everything in my power to avoid it, but people are subject to human error and I can replace both them and the money they lose. It's finite and temporary. However, employees or even business owners who diminish the reputation of the company are unforgivable. They're damaged goods who taint everything around them. You can demonstrate high quality and build up the brand's trust for decades only to have it ruined in a blink of an eye by any representative of the organization. When this happens you lose current customers, and possibility of them upselling or cross-selling. You lose future referrals, and you won't reactivate them as former customers. That's a whole lot of loss because someone tarnished your reputation.

The saying goes "hire slow and fire fast." Well, the moment that you screw up my money by contributing to a bad reputation, you're gone. You're the decision maker now. When everyone else has moved on to a different company, you're going to be the one standing there holding up the sign for new customers. When they see that your Google review sucks because someone you liked and once trusted ruined your reputation, no one is going to stop and ask you if it's true.

There is no excuse for not providing the best customer service and professionalism that you possibly can. Expect those you employ to do the same. If they can't do it, fire fast. We pray that our businesses will remain open well after we are dead and gone, but for right now, we need to make the most money possible. That means getting rid of the dead weight, no matter who they are.

Chapter 7
Creating A WOW Team

Ladies and gentlemen, I introduce to you Dr. Talonda Thomas. Self-proclaimed diva. Successful business woman. You name it, I'm it! I rightfully should have been a high school dropout since I got knocked up at 16 years old and was too hard-headed to have the abortion everyone begged me to get. I busted my butt and graduated high school early, earned a PhD by age twenty-seven. I've run half-marathons, won national awards in business, and can make the boys eat out of my hand but I'm nothing without my team. Not a damn thing.

I was at a crossroads a few years ago. I had been working closely with my mentor, and she was grooming me to take over her job. This was a big position. Great money but crazy hours. I didn't really want it, but I felt like it would be a slap in her face if I didn't go for it. The first interview was with the top two leaders for this organization. It went exceptionally well because, well, I know how to make the room stop and listen. The second callback interview was a bit more cumbersome. The seven-person panel went around and around asking me questions that I didn't feel like answering. I had become bored. You see, prepping for the interview was taking away from my time growing my OWN business.

Somehow, I made it past the second round and got invited to the third and final round with the head of the organization. I spent weeks preparing what to wear and say, and how to conduct myself, which was somehow quite intimidating. It's not as if my mentor had not prepared me.

The day of the interview, I took the afternoon off from work to go home and prepare. I wore a pinstriped suit that cost way too much from Macy's. A perfectly primed white blouse underneath and my hair perfectly pinned. I felt like a million bucks because I knew that I was ready for my big interview with the head honcho.

As I stepped out of my car to go into the interview, my heel hit the curb the wrong way and my coffee splashed all over my blouse. "Damn it!" I yelled. Coffee was everywhere. I only had about twenty minutes until I needed to check in at the interview, so I ran into a convenience store and begged them to use their bathroom to clean up. I quickly got myself together and jumped in the car to head for my interview. The music school was opening in fifteen minutes and my part-time front desk lady was out sick today, so I figured I'd call the teachers and make sure that everything was all set. It was at that moment that I got a text—a teacher wouldn't be able to come in to teach, with students scheduled to begin arriving in less than ten minutes. Meanwhile, I'm pulling up to my interview. How the hell am I supposed to find a substitute and solve this problem in eight minutes?

Tears started streaming down my face but not quite as fast as the sweat was dripping down my back. This was the exact reason that I didn't need to take on a new position that would take up all my time. I already had a company to take care of. Yet I'm sitting here drenched in sweat. My hair is now unpinned. Everything is coming undone! Literally, who goes to an interview starving with her stomach growling? I was a mess!

I started walking into the interview with the weight of the world on my shoulders, thinking about the angry customers pulling up to the music school while I'm in here trying to impress *the man.* They would be pissed for sure. Needless to say, I blew the interview.

It was the best day ever.

When they called me in to break the news to me that I wasn't getting the job, they had no idea about the relief that I felt. Getting that position would've been equivalent to a death sentence—at least for my business. They waited for my tears and asked if I was okay. Somehow, it didn't look like they believed that I was *perfectly just fine* without the new additional responsibilities. There is one thing that I learned from my interviewing experience. I needed a team of people to help me get my life together.

I didn't want to live in a way that gave me *barely* enough time to make it to my appointments or *almost* enough time to get things done in my day. I needed someone who could keep me in line with what I'm supposed to be doing and be there for my customers to give them the WOW experience that I simply didn't have time to handle. These people have changed my life into the type of life that makes me want to get up and smile every single day.

My WOW Team

You will need help on the path to reaching your goals. Companies with employees have distinct advantages over solopreneurs when it comes to achieving success. First, having a team of employees allows for the division of labor and specialization, enabling everyone to focus on their specific strengths and responsibilities. This leads to increased productivity as tasks can be delegated and shared among team members.

My team covers everything in my life from the inside-out, so I'll introduce them in that order. They handle everything from my home to my business, and most importantly, my sanity. Each of them works hand in hand although they do not all know each other. They were all hand selected after someone else screwed up at the job I needed completed. I had to go through dozens of people who cost me years and thousands of dollars until I found the right team. And although they're all right for right now, it's vital to update your team if they ever are not aligned with where you're headed.

Meet Khalilah

My health must be a top priority, so I'd like to introduce you to Khalilah first. Khalilah is my personal trainer. She stands tall and lean with glistening skin and the hair of a goddess. I can tell she takes pride in herself. And luckily, I found Khalilah by accident. At the end of 2016, I committed myself to a better lifestyle for the upcoming year. At almost 250 pounds, I was starting to have incredible leg and back pain. I would visit orthopedic professionals, chiropractors, and general practitioners with little success.

Running has always been a passion of mine, but no matter how much I ran I couldn't get off the pounds, and exercise became very difficult. I ran my last half marathon at 242 pounds, and it was unbearable. There were some days during that winter that I could barely walk.

The weight was literally weighing me down physically, emotionally, and in my business. I hid behind my big hair and big earrings all the time. Finally, after a few months with a nutritionist and working with my doctor, I decided to hire a trainer at my gym. Best part was that he was hot! I figured that I at least deserved the eye candy for working so hard day in and day out. Well, my trainer broke my cardinal rule of stealing my time. I would pause my work and race down the highway to meet this sexy beast for an hour. Dressed and pumped—I'm ready to get sweaty! Sadly, the worker at the front tells me that he's not here, so I text him. Guess who forgot about my session? Who could forget *me*? Ugh!

This happened not once, not twice, but three times. I angrily told him that I no longer needed him and complained to the manager of the gym about how unacceptable this was. "My time is valuable!" were words I either yelled inside or outside of my head.

"Don't leave. You have to work out," spoke the words of an angel.

She didn't know that I was incapable of working out while angry or mentally distracted. That angel was Khalilah. She took the time to figure out what I needed that day and has been working me out ever since. Over the past two years, I have lost almost one hundred pounds and lifted more weight than I ever thought was possible. I look in the mirror and see the powerful woman who I always felt was deep within. My schedule makes it almost impossible to see Khalilah for our twice-a-week sessions, but personal fitness and health are priorities.

If I'm not well, my business can't grow. When I work with Khalilah, she can sense when I'm bogged down with crazy things happening within my company simply by looking at my posture. She stops me and tells me to either focus and work out right or not to work out at all. Damn. That's what I need. That's what *we* need.

I inhale, listen to her every word in between our moments of laughter that make me forget about the outside world, and then I leave to conquer all. We all need a Khalilah or someone who will push us physically. I will pay for this service over any McDonald's or Starbucks because our personal health is the heartbeat of our businesses. At least find a friend or colleague who will make you commit to workouts with them. Through workouts, I've become very close with colleagues who I would never have befriended in years past.

Working out with others can significantly increase the likelihood of success in achieving workout goals. One key reason is the power of accountability. When individuals exercise in a group setting, there is a sense of camaraderie, making it easier to stay consistent and dedicated to the workout routine. Additionally, working out with others creates an element of healthy competition, pushing individuals to push their limits and strive for better performance. The social aspect of group workouts also creates a positive environment where individuals can share tips, exchange experiences, and celebrate milestones together, fostering a sense of community and encouragement. Find someone who will make you accountable for your health and will walk the journey with you.

Meet Adriana

Adriana and I met back when my oldest son first began playing football. Our sons would plow down the field making us hope with each play that they wouldn't get hurt. Adriana was especially sensitive to this, a quality that I came to love about her. In every manner of her existence, she was a caregiver and nurturer. One conversation with her would make you feel like you had just received a professional massage that soothed you to the point of sleep. She was also reassuring and assertive. A gorgeous Latina whom all the husbands noticed, staring just a second too long.

When I opened my business, she was kind enough to work for me. She was my very first front desk receptionist, and she molded that position for the many people who have held it since she left. But Adriana has many other talents. Along with being a writer and a yoga instructor, she is an amazing culinary arts expert and has once again taken the load off my shoulders by using her passion to free up some of my time by providing my family with nutritious and amazing meals.

You're probably thinking, who the hell actually gets a cook? I'm not Beyoncé or someone with a personal chef. I am a hardworking mother and entrepreneur who hates cooking. It was easier to throw a meal together when it was just my boys and me, but now that my family is blended, it's me and six guys. I don't mean little guys. I mean big 'ole football playing teens and college age guys. Nonetheless, I don't have much time to suffer through figuring out what to cook.

I choose to create the life I want and live it on purpose.

If cooking is something that I don't have time for, don't enjoy doing, or I determine that I could be spending time making money instead of in the kitchen, I'm not cook! I ran the math to figure out how to afford this extra luxury and determined that I needed to gain a certain amount of clients to afford Adriana cooking for me, and believe me, she is worth every dime and more!

Adriana creates meals that are healthy and delicious. Everyone in my household eats pretty well since they are student athletes. Adriana makes wholesome meals that I never even thought about! My mama is from Mississippi, and we were taught to put sugar in everything including your green beans. *Believe me*, I needed help with healthy cooking! Best of all, Adriana packages up food for me to bring to work. Ding, ding, ding . . . I didn't even need to get those two new clients! I can afford Adriana just because now I'm saving on the money I use to spend going out to lunch. Meanwhile, I get to enjoy food from her garden since God knows, I'll never take the time to plant one for myself.

Cleanliness Is Next to Godliness

Cleanliness is next to Godliness, at least that's what my mom would say. Please just don't let her look inside my car! Again, cleaning is not one of those things that I spend a lot of time doing. My boyfriend and I have five sons between us. I don't think you want a visual on what the bathrooms look like sometimes. Maira is currently the lovely woman who cleans my house. I'm sure this may change to someone else over time, but she does a great job.

Two things that I have learned about the need for a cleaner: it's a terrible idea for business owners to spend time scrubbing down the crown molding in their homes when they should be making money, and I can focus a whole lot better with a clean space. First, it removes some of the guilt that makes you feel that you need to stop being preoccupied with your work because the house is already clean. You may be thinking, what's the big deal with me mopping my floors?

Well, it just simply isn't congruent with the lifestyle that I'm trying to create. It doesn't make sense for me to have a million-dollar business and spend time scrubbing out my tub and toilet when there are so many things that I could be doing to fill the money pipeline. Be sure to check out Dan Kennedy's thoughts on behaviors that are congruent with making money within his book on wealth attraction.

Similarly, I recommend hiring a cleaner for your business, and I don't mean vacuum girl, whom you'll read more about later in this book. If you have the option to have staff spending time getting the next sale versus cleaning, make sure they are free to get that sale. Years ago, I would drive to my music school on my lunch breaks from my regular job with just enough time to dust, scrub the bathroom, sweep, mop, vacuum, and be drenched in sweat as I arrived back at work. Not only was it wasteful of my time but it was not good for my health to constantly be racing up and down the streets to try and wear all the hats in my business.

The incredibly successful entrepreneur and well-known shark Barbara Corcoran of NBC's Shark Tank said "make sure you pick good people to build your business with, as they'll determine 80 percent of your success. This fact should both excite you and petrify you. It's petrifying because there will be some lame hires along the way. The employee who never shows up for their first shift or who steals from the company. It could even be the employee who fakes an accident to sue you or simply always promises to return your customers calls but never does. People are people. But if you allow yourself to get good at reading people to determine if they have good character, then your success will explode.

Meet Hajara Musa

About five years back, I decided that I wanted to live more naturally by giving up hair relaxers, which many African American women use to keep their hair straight. I did what many people call the *big chop* and cut off all my hair that had been processed with the hair straightener because I was empowered by a series of YouTube videos. I cut all my hair off by myself and got ready to look in the mirror at the new, beautiful me.

When I looked in the mirror, I was horrified. The beautiful image I was expecting was not the one I saw.

Instead, I noticed that my hairline was uneven, and my forehead felt much bigger than it ever did before. Somehow, I needed to go to work the next day looking professional and remotely close to my glamorous self. I frantically started calling around to see if any hair shops were open, but it was only 8:00 a.m. on a Sunday morning. To my rescue, a woman named Hajara Musa was already awake and up on her grind when she answered the phone. It was then that she set off a series of moments for me to feel successful on the outside for years to come.

Over the years, I've learned that **it doesn't make any sense to do your best and work your hardest if you don't feel successful on both the inside and outside**. If you don't feel confident, then you'll never accomplish the goals you set. Likewise, if you want your customers to respect your work and know that you are the authority in your sector, then you must look the part, whatever that might mean for your field. In my profession, I hold several events where performers are dressed in their formal gowns, and I'm scheduled to be the host of the evening. However, anyone who knows me understands that I am the worst at doing hair and makeup.

Hajara Musa is a stylist in New York City who immediately struck me the first time I met her. She was adorned in the most stylish fashion. She didn't look overdone or highly involved in designer clothing. Instead, she looked like her fashion sense was all about who she was. Elegant, regal, refined. I approached her and told her that I needed a style with extensions since I had just chopped off my hair unevenly and needed to look great for an event the following day. The problem was, it's pretty hard to braid in extensions when you have almost no hair to braid. I had done *that* much damage and was begging Hajara to save me. She agreed to *make it work*.

This new mortal savior of mine wasn't just beautiful, but she was willing to work with me whenever I needed her, willing to make the impossible happen, and most of all, hungry to be successful in her business.

When I saw this, I knew that I would have to keep her in my life. Now I know what to do when I'm in a pinch and need to be styled quickly. I call Hajara! She hooks me up for every event no matter when or where. She offers "on the go" services that help me keep up with my busy lifestyle and quite frankly, I don't want to play Carnegie Hall unless I've got Hajara or someone like her on my team with the hookup because I am my brand and my brand includes how I look and feel.

Meet Vanessa

There are times when I wish I could meet a male version of Vanessa. I mean, I love my boyfriend and we've been together a long time, but Vanessa rocks my world and she knows it! Every business needs a powerhouse. Someone who can handle the toughest clients and bring in every sale that comes their way. Vanessa is the office manager of my business, and I like to refer to her as the missing part of my brain.

When she came to my company, I sent her away immediately for customer service training, and she returned as a sales maniac. Each year she grew profits, she kept the staff together since I don't work on premises, and most of all, she holds me accountable for making sure that my marketing goals are making the phones ring.

Each day, an email is sent to me telling me what our current numbers are for the month and how far we are from our goal. Vanessa nails it every single time. She hires staff for me, fights our battles with vendors, lets people know what Dr. Thomas will and will not accept (in my absence), and has made the success of my business high on her priority list. Working in my business is not something I desire. I love seeing my clients, but my time is much better used elsewhere, and there is no beach inside my business. The only way to set up your daily activities freely without being present at your business is to groom someone who will care for it, sprinkle fertilizer on it every day, and watch that baby grow!

Find someone who can grow your business daily, because you can't work *on* your business if you're working *in* your business. Otherwise, make sure that there is someone else to grow your business if you plan on working *in* it. But you've got to choose.

Give Me an Accountant and Attorney or Close My Shop!

September 2016 was a wonderful time for my company. Daily operations were running smoothly, we were soon to hit 400 clients, and we were about to celebrate our fifth business anniversary in operation. This was MAJOR! My team sat and planned the details of our community party. I focused on who we would invite and how we would celebrate our customers all winter long. November 6th was the anniversary date, and I was *ready*. I had finally made it! My business would not be one of the failures in less than five years!

It was November 1st, and I was at home sneaking some of my son Julien's Halloween candy from the night before. Underneath the bag of candy was the mail. I lifted up the bag, and there it was. The letter that I had been terrified to receive since the day I opened for business. It was a notice for an audit. Word in the community of music school owners was that this particular agency had it out for businesses in my field and to always be prepared.

I wasn't ready. I wasn't prepared at all.

It hit me like a ton of bricks. My stomach felt like an alien was trying to climb out from my insides, and I broke into uncontrollable tears as I sat down on the couch. How was I supposed to prepare for an audit? Immediately I picked up the phone and called my accountant.

"Mr. Franks office, how may I help you?" the sweet voice on the other end said.

"Hi, this is Talonda Thomas. I was wondering if Mr. Franks is available."

"No, I'm sorry. He isn't available. Can I take a message?" she explained.

"Yes, please let him know that I called and that it's urgent."

She said, "Sure, he's quite busy filing returns, but I'll make sure that he calls you back."

It's been twenty-one months and I'm still waiting on that call to be returned.

I emailed my accountant to let him know that I needed his help with the audit. In the meanwhile, I asked a few friends for attorney referrals since I secretly had never hired an attorney to consistently handle any of my business affairs. I spoke to a wonderful attorney who informed me that he had successful defended audits like mine, but that I would be looking at a $5,000 deposit and a total of about $20,000.

Twenty thousand dollars? Holy crap! I don't have $20,000. I can still feel the tears burning down my face. Meanwhile, I called my mom for a listening ear, and she says, "Hmph, I sure hope you're handling your business. Don't play with the government." I reassured her, "No mom, if you're in business for long enough, you can expect an audit, and I haven't done anything wrong." Unlike many people I know, I actually *do* claim cash and run my place by the books. My audit was scheduled for the day before Thanksgiving.

I knew I had a lot to be thankful for, but it sure didn't feel like it. The five-year celebration had been canceled. I felt like my whole life was temporarily canceled. As the weeks went by, I added up the cost of everything that the auditor was requesting. It would cost me almost $1,000 to request from the bank copies of old canceled checks from previous years, and the list went on and on. My accountant never called or emailed me back, and I couldn't afford the attorney. I was on my own, but I was also sure that I was the best person to speak on behalf of my business. Again, I knew that I was doing everything by the books.

The morning of the audit, I had to take a personal day off from my regular nine-to-five job so that I could meet with the auditor. My stomach was again in knots. I

Screw the Business Plan

had more documents laid out for him than I even knew existed for my business. Well, about an hour later, a middle-aged man walked through my door. He looked like a mathematician, and we small-talked for a while. I thought, "Surely, this guy is reasonable."

After a half hour into our conversation, he stated that his agency would like to charge me thousands of dollars because they believe they are entitled to the additional amount. He looked through one payroll period for one employee and said, "I don't really need to go through all of this."
Wait. Did he just say that he is not going to bother to check out my documents?

I spent the month preparing, gathering, and printing everything for his disposal. I pled my case to the auditor, and he informed me that his agency has the ability to simply decide that they disagree with me and that he didn't believe that I ran my business the way that I explained.

Again, wait. You don't believe me? Does this guy want to interview my staff? Tell me what to do or what part of my soul I have to sell to make you understand!

He left. Just like that.

A month later I received the bill for $3,120. It wasn't the amount of money that bothered me. It was the fact that they could now choose any number they wanted me to pay at any time and for any reason. I felt violated, like I never had a chance. Like this person was sent to come raise havoc for my business just because it was my turn. This was NOT in my business plan.

That was the moment that I learned I will never do business without a reliable accountant and attorney on retainer. I don't want to ever operate another day without these two people. Work out a deal with these people to pay them monthly. The day will come when you need them if you're lucky to be in business long enough.

One of the biggest reasons why people in business don't spend money retaining an attorney and an accountant to use beyond tax time is because the idea of such a large expense can literally suck the breath out of your body. Family and friends don't always *get it,* so they'll usually just tell you to handle your business so you don't get locked up, because like my mom would say, "The government don't play!" The bad news is that my mama is right! Every agency that can squeeze money out of your business will, in fact, do just that. The great news is that you're a creative entrepreneur, so make a way! When I first opened my business location and needed an attorney to review my lease, I thought of all the attorneys I knew. One of the best lawyers I knew was so excited that I was opening this business that she did the work pro-bono and asked me to pay it forward. I did just that.

You can afford the attorney or accountant. All you need is the faith and the right math!

Funding Your Dream Team

One of the best lessons that I have ever learned as a new entrepreneur was that **money is made through math not emotion**. Our emotions are what drive us to overspend, to try and create a program or product for our businesses that no one is will want to purchase or is even interested in using, or even worse, it keeps us from being creative because our emotions drive us to focus on everything except our businesses. In business, the opposite of emotion is math. I've never been great at math. Not in sixth grade, not even with a PhD.

After three painful years of trying to get my business's math to make sense, I attended a private conference with my multimillionaire business coach. He promised us the opportunity to stand up in front of our peers and ask for help solving a problem. When it came to my turn, I stood before these business owners and told them that I didn't have the time to grow my business while continuing my full-time job. Yet, I wasn't quite financially ready to leave my job.

I stood in the front of the freezing conference room with a blank easel. My mentor, seemingly ready to work quickly, abruptly jumped out of his seat and took a sip of water. He walked over and said, "Okay, let's do the math." It was then that he walked me through the math of determining what I needed and how to get it. Here's what it looked like:

What did I need: To afford a full-time office manager

What would it cost weekly? 40 hours/week × $16 = $640 + approx. $100 in taxes = $740/week

What would be the monthly cost? 160 hours/month × $16/hour starting = 2,560 + 400 (approximate taxes) = $2,900

How could I afford this new expense? Determine how many clients it would take to make $2,900.

My monthly profit from each new client at the time: $65
How many clients it would take: 45

The questions then became, "Do I have $2,900 to spare each month to have someone else come in and grow my business?" and "How long would it take to acquire 45 new clients?" Most importantly, how long would it take this new manager to sign up 45 new clients to pay for her own salary?

The answer was easy. Since I still had my day job, I could easily take $2,900 of my current profit and pay to bring on a manager. Then, I would expect her to quickly register those 45 clients to pay for herself.

I went home immediately and put out an advertisement for a full-time manager. I felt so official! I could actually pay someone's salary and get someone committed because they are full-time. I'd increase the pay over time, and she would grow my business! Waaah-hoo!

At that time, I was hanging around 180 clients per month. It wasn't long before this superstar manager brought us to 200, 250, 300, and now . . . more than 500 clients! I'd say that she paid for herself. She loves her job and bonuses, and I've been given a raise that was triple what I was making previously.

All of a sudden, the math made sense.

A WOW team will change your business, grow your business, improve your health, and set your business apart from the rest. As I said before, one of the biggest mistakes you can ever make when learning how to run your business is spending too much time working *in* your company instead of *on* your company. It's the same reason why many business owners get a slow (but steady) start, and then find it difficult to grow. Their time is being spent running errands for the company, answering calls, providing the actual services, managing the company books, and the endless other tasks when in fact there is only one thing that you should be focusing on—MARKETING YOUR BUSINESS. Well, what if you could delegate those tasks to a person?

One concern is obviously that the money isn't there to afford it. The other is that you should spend a small amount of time working on these tasks so that you can learn what it takes to effectively run your business. But don't stay in that situation. Do the math and leap! Determine what "WOW" team member you need to give you more time to market your business and do the things you want.

Who is one "WOW" team member that you need?

_____

Do the math below.

Hours/week_____ × Hourly pay $_____ = $_____

Total from above_____ + taxes_____ = _____

Total weekly cost: _____

How much would it cost you per month? _____

Here are the key questions to ask yourself. Do you have that monthly amount available to spare right now? If not, can you start smaller?

How many more clients or product sales would you need to pay this monthly expense?

Can you make it happen? The answer is a resounding **yes**! You can!
  The difference between staff and a WOW team is in the way that they've been trained and the excellence that they produce. Before I put my team together, I was running all over the place. Staples, the hardware store, grocery stores, you name it, and I did it. I was even racing over to my business during lunchtime while I still had a traditional job and yet I was also cleaning toilets so that they'd be clean for the first customer. Do you think my staff cared? No.

  My staff was there to do a job and get a paycheck. The WOW team has two simple purposes. We get clients, and we keep clients. Once I taught my staff that everything we do is to support those two initiatives, it became easier for them to understand what they needed to do. Every interaction that we have with a client must attract new clients and wow our current clients so much that they'll want to stay with us forever. In the meanwhile, they'll refer all their friends, too! Most importantly, every great leader has to realize that they can't put together an incredible business without the help of others while still maintaining health and sanity. For that reason, you've got to find members of your team who can support every area of your life.

Train Your Team for the Lifestyle You Want

  My grandmother always said to "start out like you could hold out!" Basically, that meant to train people early how you expect to be treated. Most people use this mindset with their new spouses. You want to show them what things that you like and what things that you won't stand for in a relationship. This is exactly how you have to treat your WOW team. You can't expect excellence unless you teach people what you find to be excellent.

My gym instructor was constantly changing his availability at the last minute. I told him I needed a new trainer because my lifestyle isn't set up to be flexible with other people's schedules. My office staff walk into work six minutes late after arriving on time to work every day for their first two months in the position and guess what happens. I write them up so that they know I am adamant on policies being followed. There is some wiggle room, I'm not heartless . . . but I am unemotional when it comes to following policy. I need my people to know that the job I pay for can't be completed if they're not even there.

Let's look a bit deeper at this.

I want the people around me to understand my lifestyle. They need to be trained on how I want my time and businesses treated. For example, I don't like being bothered with many phone calls or emails. Other than often being distracted and a huge victim of *monkey brain* (Google it), I simply hate being disturbed by conversations that don't bring me joy or make me money! For those reasons, I train my staff to handle nonemergency situations without my permission, and only call me between the hours of 1:00 p.m. and 3:00 p.m. when I will turn on my brain for handling other people's problems. It's not just them though, I ask people on my voicemail not to leave me voice messages because I hate listening to them. Most important people feel comfortable texting or emailing me, but don't dare mistakenly text me and not be a friend!

You must treat people to honor your boundaries and time. This isn't about being polite. This is about setting up your team to make you successful, productive, and wealthy so you can enjoy the lifestyle that you created. Now, the person without small children who just has a little dog named Rover and a sweet neighbor who calls once in a while to make sure that you're still alive may want a whole lot more action than I do. They want the calls, and they want the control of making all the decisions. And they don't mind getting the call during the middle of dinner with the in-laws either! If that's your desired lifestyle, then you would train your WOW team differently.

Get Ready for Replacements

While starting my first business, I fluttered with excitement hiring my first receptionist, Adriana. You read a bit about her culinary arts skills on my WOW team. At the time, she happened to be just a good friend of mine and was also one of the mothers from my son's football team. We often had great laughs, and her vibes made me feel like everyone would love to be around her. Adriana was tall, exotic looking, had long flowing hair and hips that every mom who entered my business wanted to know how to get!

I hired Adriana cheap, and she helped me get my business off the ground. Soon after, I realized that I needed to bring on more staff. And then another, and another, and so on. As I raked up a good handful of front office staff, some began to part ways. It was usually on great terms. I mean, I started this business with zero managerial experience. My first receptionist could be found at the front desk brushing her teeth, but I was getting a lot a good out of her unorthodox ways.

After Adriana left the office, so did the next one. I had to let go of another one because she showed me that she didn't care about her work. The next had to be let go because she refused to come in on time. The next quit because she was written up and her millennial heart couldn't handle the criticism that she had done something wrong. Each and every time one person left, we found someone even better than the last person. The new hires tended to be better because we learned from our mistakes with the last person and figured out ways to train them better or tweak the position based on their skills.

The problem came one January as I looked down at all the W-2s that I was mailing out. How could I possibly have gone through this many receptionists this year?

The teaching faculty at my music school must be realizing that the staff in my front office was starting to maneuver their way through our rotating door. One person in, another on the way in, another on the way out. I started to feel like things were inconsistent and that my customers would start getting angry if I didn't get my crap together. Then I looked up at my current staff rocking out our sales, looked at our numbers for the year noticing that we grew by 95 percent that year, and yelled "NEXT ONE UP"!

Everyone is so consumed by their *feelings* and connections with the people in their businesses that they will allow even the worst people to stay on working, even if they are not the right fit. Then when it's time to cut their losses, many entrepreneurs will damn near wallow in a grieving period wondering what they did wrong as a boss or how the ex-employee is going to survive without them.

Trust me, they will get by just fine. You didn't pop them out as a baby. You didn't groom them and teach them all their skills and habits as a child, and you will not allow them to waste your money and efforts to grow your business. Next one up.

Chapter 8
THE ART OF LIVING

If your life is anything like mine was, you might have been a walking disaster. Throughout college, my coworkers would tell me that if it weren't for bad luck, I'd have no luck at all. I believed they were right. Things were *always* going wrong for me. There was always some mix-up that didn't benefit me, or I'd end up in an accident due to faulty mechanics. You name it, and I've had it. I even had my longtime boyfriend and the father of my child run off with one of my twelfth-grade high school students when I was eight months pregnant. I'm telling you, I've been around the block.

For a long time, it felt like life was just happening to me. I was simply a spectator with poor seats. It was never fair and whatever I had in time or money, it was never enough. By the time I was twenty-one, I found myself hospitalized with what they believed had been a stroke, leaving me unable to speak clearly, walk normally, or write properly for days. I knew exactly what it was. Stress. Chaos. It was my lack of ability to get everything crammed into one day's work and the crashing feeling that tomorrow would be overwhelming once again. Not with the things that I loved to do, but with the mundane items on my never-ending to-do list.

Sadly, I continued to live that way for another decade, pressuring myself through goals without the proper timing or mentorship. None of those days were fun but I got all the accolades and fame for high productivity and *killing it* at work. It wasn't until my ninth year of full-time teaching and simultaneously running my company that I realized enough was enough. I was cooped up with my laptop and my kids weren't experiencing half the things that my friend's kids were. We had more assets than many, but that meant diddly-squat when I realized that my nine-year-old didn't even know how to ride a bike. What the heck was I doing writing a Facebook advertisement when my kid couldn't ride a bike? That was my moment.

Designed Living

There's a point in everyone's life when they experience an awakening. Some people call it a second puberty, mid-life crisis, or just "waking up." It's the moment when we realize that we haven't done the things that we've hoped to accomplish or fulfill dreams that we always had in mind. I must say that I was extremely moved by Daymond John's book, *Rise and Grind*, which encouraged me to put to paper my process of living. A process that many people live out in different forms and others simply laugh at. Once I read his book's opening quote by the Dalai Lama, I knew I had to put my experience on paper.

> "Man surprised me most about humanity. Because he sacrifices his health in order to make money. Then he sacrifices money to recuperate his health. And then is so anxious about the future that he does not enjoy the present, the result being that he does not live in the present or the future. He lives as if he is never going to die, and then dies having never really lived."
>
> **-Dalai Lama**

The Dalai Lama was talking about me and *my* life before I taught myself a method to not only *get through* but to thrive. For me, this process is called Designed Living. I also like to think of it as the *art of living*. Designed Living is a non-panicked, predetermined, and conscious decision to design your life based on what you love doing, no matter what others say.

Let's look deeper.

It's a plan to live every day as if you deserve all your greatest desires and to work toward each of your goals and desires without the need for a crisis to catapult you to getting what you want. Designed Living gives you the joy of determining *what* and *who* makes us happy, and then designing our daily schedule around them. This decision is conscious.

You're the captain who gets to guide what direction you're going in. This conscious decision-making takes away phrases like "one day, I'd like to . . . ," and "must be nice . . . I wish I could......"

A few months back, my sister told me that my mom was going off on a motherly tangent, saying, "I wish Talonda would settle down, find a husband, and could live the way that she said she used to dream about." At the time, I was vacationing in Aruba. Completely carefree. My sister told my mother, "I think that she *is* living her dream." You see, Designed Living has nothing to do with what others want or expect you to do. It's 100 percent based on how *you* want to spend your time. For me, I have four areas that I design my life around.

The first is health. Health is before anything else because without good health, you've got nothing else. For this reason, I start my day focused on exercise and food that is good for my body. By no means is this easy. I spent most of my life swaying between 170 and 250 pounds. I only made it under 170 when I was completely starving myself, throwing up into buckets like a bulimic teenager, and running several miles a day on fumes. That was not joy, and it certainly wasn't good health, but it was all I knew. Now, I've learned to address my weight issues with a nutritionist and a high-protein, low-carb diet. I also learned to love lifting weights. As a result, I've lost and kept off over ninety pounds. These days, I focus on what makes my body *feel good* and put more of that into my life. That's a priority to me, so it comes first.

The second area that I have designed into my life is the fulfillment of my income responsibility. This means that I've got to make the money to fund my livelihood and the activities that I enjoy. These tasks support my family and yet are sometimes the hardest to force myself to get done. For this reason, I've always got to get them completed in the morning. Every single morning requires me to look at the health of my finances to bring in more money. Personally, for my business, it may be setting up a networking event, a social media advertisement, or simply responding to emails from my customers. Nonetheless, these items are important and get my second priority each day. They are designed into my business, and I don't expect for them to get done on their own.

In addition, I don't commit more than 25 percent of my day on average to this task. Of course, there are days when there are full-day events that are bringing me in money, but on an average day, I spend 25 percent of my time on this area. As you design your day, consider how you fulfill your work responsibilities since they are the ones that will afford you to meet personal goals such travel, furthering your education, or buying that brand new car that you've been dreaming about for way too long.

The third area of my life where my time is next spent each day is with my family. This could be fulfilling family obligations like attending a function for a distant cousin, but most routinely this includes hanging out with my sons and spending time with my boyfriend on our date nights. This area is extremely important and often the area that gets neglected most. However, family and work have to have some sort of a balance even if you're spending half the time trying to balance the seesaw.

The fourth area that I choose to design into my schedule is my hobbies. Designed Living requires me to determine what I love to do and the things I've always wished to try. Those items now get put onto my calendar. I've designed my time and the allocation of my income to be spent traveling to the places that I've wanted to visit. Music and jogging are my passions that I choose to put into my schedule. Writing music, singing, visiting islands of the Caribbean, and so much more. Whatever it is that you love to do or items that you hope to acquire and enjoy, there isn't any use in waiting around. You don't know if you'll be here next week, so make a plan and set a date to go get it. If it's a new pool or new wife, I firmly believe that we must go get what we want. It may take time, and we may need to rearrange the other areas of our lives to get the design that's perfect for us, but we have to constantly and purposely be molding our routines to be in line with what we desire to have and how we desire to live.

One of the hardest decisions for people is the choice of how they want to live life. What *they* enjoy doing. Even harder is determining *who* they want to do these activities with. Believe me it's not easy. I've had to pull the strings on some friendships and relationships that I had for years. Nonetheless, it's time to determine who and what makes your cut list.

Designing *Your Life*

1. What exercise activity can you commit to daily?

_____

What time can you commit to completing it by?

_____

2. What work activities provide for you and your family?

_____

_____

What time can you commit to completing it by each day?

_____

3. What activities do you want to complete with your friends or family?

_____

What time frame do you want to designate for this in your routine?

_____

4. What activities do you *need* to complete with your friends or family?

_____

Who can you delegate some of these tasks to?

_____

5. Think back to your happiest moments—childhood, early adulthood, any of the times you've been happy and free. What activities did you enjoy doing most?

_____

_____

_____

Where can you add these into your monthly or daily calendar?

_____

_____

6. What items have you wanted for so long? Not just a little, but you can see yourself with them.

_____

_____

Screw the Business Plan

_____

7. Where have you always wanted to travel?

_____

_____

_____

8. When would an actual date be that you can go to one of these places? ("Never" isn't a viable answer.)

_____

***

Areas to seek help with as you mold your new schedule:

Current health concerns_____

_____

_____

Desires to change job_____

_____

_____

Desires to change relationship partners_____

_____

_____

New educational goals_____

_____

Friends who deserve more of your time_____

_____

_____

Friends or family who have been holding your back_____

_____

_____

      Of all the things life provides us, the desire for change and growth will be impossible to avoid. Choose to live how you want. If you want more, you have to do more. But most of all, design the plan for your routines, your calendar, and where you're heading. Don't forget to choose the right people to come with you.

SECTION III
THE DAILY GRIND

*"Excellence is the next five minutes...
Forget the long term.
Make the next five minutes rock!"*

-Tom Peters

Chapter 9
PRODUCTIVITY

Productivity is a word that gets thrown around but is misunderstood by new business owners. The word itself is the state of producing something. That means you need a whole lot to show for the work that you're doing. The average entrepreneur who is stalled on items like their business plan are stuck writing, planning, and creating items that produce nothing. There's no outcome, there's no money made, there is just a bunch of unusable pieces of paper that no one will ever see. If I showed you my original business folder in my laptop, you'd laugh hysterically. There are hundreds of files that I've never actually needed.

On the flip side, the very successful entrepreneurs are rocking it out. They don't stop moving, and their breaks are spent mingling with the right people to help take them to the next level. They don't feel like their success has earned them breaks until they actually *break through*, start making deals, and grabbing cash in the process.

Setting Up Your Day for Success

Many new entrepreneurs can be found up early in the morning and awake well after their family has gone to sleep. Time is spent studying how to make more money and how to finally get that new product or service off the ground. Worn out and disheveled, we spend so much wasted time bouncing from one thought to the next. Each item on our to-do list is reactive of what's going on around us, and we fail to build a schedule that allows us to be productive.

One of the key ingredients to success is figuring out what activities are required every day to bring in one new customer and determining what activities in your life make you most productive and happy.

There are several routines that successful people all keep the same. One of them is taking care of the hard stuff money-making items early in the morning. Build your routine around what's most important even if it's not one of your favorite things to do. That means that Facebook and Instagram may have to wait until later in the day. Don't allow anyone to interrupt your morning routine and try to stick with it. At times when you're first starting a business, it may feel like everyone around you is out having fun and you're dedicating more hours than you feel are healthy toward getting your project completed. The truth of the matter is that someone is always out there hustling, and you've got to be one of them if you want to live better.

Entrepreneurs tend to lead very high frequency lives. We're constantly putting out one fire, while dealing with an angry customer in the middle of figuring out taxes, and trying to keep our employees from running off with a competitor.

It's a lot!

There are many nights when you can feel the blood pressure rising, and you're racing against the clock to get every little thing done. People are driving you nuts, interrupting your output, and things are piling up no matter how fast you work to complete them. The result is stress, and we know what stress brings.

> **"If I wake up three mornings thinking about you, and I'm not having sex with you, you've got to go."**
>
> **-Dan Kennedy**

Here are a few pieces of advice that I've learned to live by to be productive.

1. My schedule is my sanctuary, not to be disturbed.
2. Unplug from the world sometimes.
3. No social media in the morning unless it's to make money.
4. Prioritize what's important to me and schedule my day accordingly.

5. Cut out people and things that take up too much of my time.

One of the greatest challenges for business owners is to simply *keep up* with everything going on—dates things need to be done by, people we need to contact, and so much more. I've personally found that it becomes easier and easier to put things off simply because you don't want to make a rushed decision or because too many things are jumping on the plate at one time. That was until I read about the one touch rule.

According to super entrepreneur Daymond John, the One Touch Rule says that "you should act on every bill, every email, every phone message the very first time it crosses your desk…just think how much time you waste re-reading all this stuff when you eventually get around to it…successful people see it, process it, and act on it—immediately…". This rule has changed the way I handle things in life or business and that's because being decisive and taking quick action is crucial for personal growth and success. Procrastination often leads to missed opportunities, wasted time, and increased stress.

When we make timely decisions, we demonstrate our ability to prioritize and seize the moment. Decisiveness allows us to overcome fear, uncertainty, and doubt, empowering us to make progress towards our goals instead of moving at the pace of average people. It fosters a sense of momentum, propelling us forward and opening doors to new possibilities. By taking immediate massive action, we gain a competitive edge, as the world rewards those who are proactive and efficient.

I dare you to try this for one day, or even half of a day. You'll immediately feel more calm and productive. The practice of the one touch rule will give you back your sanity in just a moment's time. Instead of reading an email and trying to decide what to do with it, you're forced to be decisive and get that one email off your plate immediately.

The moment a request comes through, it gets one touch and doesn't earn the right to stay on your mind for long periods. Try this tomorrow!

OPEN LETTER TO DAYMOND JOHN

Dear Mr. John,

In the final stages of writing this book, I picked up your book *Rise and Grind*. My schedule has only recently allowed me to read as much as I would like, so I landed in Barnes & Noble, roaming around like a kid at the candy store. I grabbed your book because I was sure you had something relatable to say, and I needed some sense of normalcy or relaxation that I wasn't getting during my own writing process. I read about the one touch method you described, which instantaneously changed my daily routine.

In addition, I found your thoughts on perspective to be incredibly familiar. You wrote about Gary Vaynerchuk forcing his brain to think about something bad happening to his family in order to keep perspective. After reading this, I realized that I'm wasn't alone in this sea of entrepreneurs.

I, too, frequently and vividly, imagine my kids being hit by a car, in a car accident, or given a death sentence through illness, and find myself physically aching. My whole body in uncontrollable agony with tears flowing. I never understood why I would think of or dream these things, but now I see that this is a shared vision. It's what people feel when they work so hard every day for something or someone but knowing it can all be taken away the next moment. My most prized possessions, I couldn't even imagine. Of course, I adore my entire family but my boys—I choke at every thought of something ever happening to them.

You see, I was inspired by my boys at a very young age. I became pregnant at age 16 and was thrust into a very adult world without a single bit of adult experience. All I could do was hustle and grind daily then repeat.

My kids determine my moves. My well-being.

Many may find pregnancy at the age of 16 to be a life altering hindrance. It was my greatest blessing in life. I'd never be who I am without that *push.*

The fact that Gary Vaynerchuk can bring himself to that place as a strategy, a practice—that is incredible. For me, it comes naturally and pushes me every day, more and more.

Thank you for sharing this "mortality check" and letting us know it's simply a part of the grind. I'll forever grind for my boys and hope to one day meet you so that I can continue learning practices of such a great money mover.

Sincerely,
Dr. Talonda

*"When 99 percent of your life is your work,
either you are really bad at what you do
or you are completely off balance with the rest of
your life;
neither is something to be proud of."*

- Jérôme Jarre

Chapter 10
WORK-LIFE BALANCE

In the first few years of running my company, I developed a routine that worked for me. I went to my day job from 7:00 a.m. to 3:00 p.m., came home to abruptly begin working, and would quickly get so engulfed in my work that I would forget that the kids needed dinner made. I'd shove the fastest dinner ever into the oven, then quickly went back to working until I couldn't hold my eyes open any longer.

On weekends, I would wake up before the kids and begin grinding. Creating websites, sending out sales letters, searching for employees. You name it, I was busy doing it. By 3:00 p.m., I'd be in damn near sweats from working so hard and then go out for a run. By the time that I finally got to my kids, the day would be nearly over. I'd look on Instagram or Facebook and see all the awesome places that my friends were enjoying with their kids, and my kids were looking at me work most of the day trying to meet deadlines. This wasn't balance. This was just bad.

We can have all the goals in the world, but the number one goal for most of us is to not badly screw up our relationships with family and friends. For some strange reason, people tend to lose their minds once they realize that something has begun consuming their time and resources other than them. Regardless, none of this great life as an entrepreneur will be worth anything if we lose our family in the process.

We've all heard of trying to balance work with family time, but those of us with more than one hundred tasks in our job description know that the balancing act is more of a juggling act. Kids and spouses want our attention at the same times that we are trying to make deadlines. As I write this sentence, my significant other continues to walk into the room with the announcement that he can't believe that the movie *Matrix* came out almost twenty years ago even though this is *my* writing time. At the same time, my seventeen-year-old is calling to ask for a ride home from school and my nine-year-old is begging me to stay up later for a few more minutes with his video game. Ahhh! Instead of attempting to make these people understand how precious my time is, I've learned to nurture these relationships and provide them the best time that I've got when I'm with them.

> "Imagine life is a game in which you are juggling five balls. The balls are called work, family, health, friends, and integrity. And you're keeping all of them in the air. But one day, you finally come to understand that work is a rubber ball. If you drop it, it will bounce back. The other four balls—family, health, friends, integrity—are made of glass. If you drop one of these, it will be irrevocably scuffed, nicked, perhaps even shattered. And once you truly understand the lesson of the five balls, you will have beginnings of balance in your life."
>
> —James Patterson, *Suzanne's Diary for Nicholas*

My family and friends know my schedule, although they may often try to interfere. It's up to me to provide attention, juggle these areas, and put myself into a workspace where I can get things accomplished.

Emotional Interceptions

I'm a die-hard football fan. I never liked it as a kid but the way these teams strategize for success really reminds me a lot of business. One of the most glorious moments on Sundays is when my team catches an interception. The sunken feeling of your opponent having the ball, but luck would have it that you get the chance to steal the victory from them . . . well, that is what I have found to be the hardest part of balancing business and my everyday life with friends and family. No matter how consistently driven we are to get things done that will grow our business, there are going to be people in our lives who throw us situations that upset us, piss us off, or worry us.

The distraction could be a sick family member, broken down car that you can't afford to fix, trouble at your day job, and, really, the list is endless. Every time we get going with our plans and projects, good old problems come our way and intercept our emotions. Our emotions shouldn't matter in business, but they are the very things that block us from thinking straight when it matters most. Sometimes there isn't even a way around it.

I'm a pretty damn focused person. Living on my own, I had a great routine that was self-directed. Basically, I'd work on my business any time that I pleased. Wake up at 4:00 a.m. with a great idea while the kids were asleep, then sit on the couch with a strong cup of coffee and work. Really, all day if I felt like it. Well, when I moved in with my longtime partner, I learned very quickly that having one argument meant that I wouldn't be able to sit there and focus any further on rolling out my marketing plan for the month. My mind was too concerned with why the heck this guy is acting like a jerk and what I can do to fix it.

What I have learned is that it's okay to give myself time to be human. I can be angry with the people and situations around me for happening, but I can't get mad at how they interrupt my progress. It's up to me to find ways to clear my mind from the emotional baggage and press forward.

Creating balance in your schedule is like the process of needing a balance sheet. Our balance sheets show us how much our businesses have in assets, as well as what we owe. A successful business will never be worth having until you balance your life with your family (assets) with what you owe in time to your company. The time that is spent is a liability in your family's eyes until both areas fall in line for the betterment of both profits and quality of life.

Imagine that you're a 12-year-old boy who only sees your father when he's staring a laptop working, running off to his business to unlock the doors because a new hire overslept, or once he's ready to pass out from exhausting himself. It doesn't make the child more excited about one day taking over the family business. It causes resentment for the business and is one of the reasons why you must create level of balance between taking care of your loved ones and achieving your dreams.

Creating Balance

The great thing about working for yourself is that you can spend time working on your own projects instead of someone else's. However, this can be difficult without a rigid, inflexible schedule if you're someone like me who is accustomed to a high frequency schedule. Some of us with families and tight schedules thrive well now because we have less time to work. But the goal is not to work harder but to be smarter.

The first method to getting back some control and organization in your schedule is by blocking hourly time when no one can call you. This means you can't sleep in! Your schedule must be mapped out and you've got to commit to it. Otherwise, you'll blow your time like someone who wins the lottery or an inheritance. They blow it because they have too much of it, don't know what to do with it, and don't have it allocated.

Adjustments that I Make to My Calendar:

✓ Schedule is preplanned six months in advance
✓ 75 percent of my time is prescheduled, 25 percent is flexible
✓ Single function days (writing days, conference days,etc.)
✓ Scripted day by the hour
✓ Preplanned family trips to look forward to

While it may seem unreasonable to keep a schedule that is so strict, it's the only way for me to keep all things aligned. Here is a copy of my scripted day:

Monday-Friday
9:00 a.m.: Workout
10:00 a.m.: Review accounts and business statistics
11:00 a.m.: Focus on one area of either writing content, personal writing, staffing, consulting calls, or planning projects/events
1:00 p.m.-3:00 p.m.: Available via phone if needed

3:00 p.m.-Bedtime: Spend time with family and friends
Off on weekends

Sacrifice

Back in grad school, I developed a routine to get my dissertation written. I would do homework on my lunch break at work and begin working again when I arrived home until I passed out. Weekend mornings were spent waking up before my children, and then I'd work straight through the day. As a runner, I always felt the need to get a workout in during the morning time and would find myself damn near sweating and shaking if I didn't stop to work out by a certain time. It was because my body was conditioned to need the run. It was something that helped me continue working.

During those years, I didn't have much of a life. I had no clue what the latest television shows were, and I didn't frequent the social events that my friends would throw. Invitations were often declined, and family members were constantly convincing me that I was working too hard. They couldn't see the end goal or even what I was trying to accomplish. The results were that my dissertation took me less than a year to complete. I managed to get a work promotion and a book written around the same time, along with a business open within months.

Most people aren't willing to sacrifice everything, but a smart entrepreneur knows these are temporary stages of business. Entrepreneurs tend to have differing views about work-life balance for business owners. I'd like to believe that my views are closest to Shark Tank's Kevin O'Leary's, also known as Mr. Wonderful, and the viewpoint of Facebook Live's creator Randi Zuckerberg.

According to Kevin O'Leary, "being an entrepreneur is a state of mind. If you're going to be an entrepreneur, my thesis is that you have to sacrifice everything for some period in your life to be successful. You have to be myopic and completely focused and unbalanced in every way. Once you've achieved success, you're free to do whatever you like." This train of thought is most popular among many who have achieved great success. While I believe it's vital to outwork everyone else if you want to have a life that's different than the average person, I love how Randi Zuckerberg (formerly of Facebook) provided in her book entitled Pick Three. I had the opportunity to interview Randi on her book's topic and to find out how the sister of Mark Zuckerberg and the creator of Facebook Live could possibly have balance in her life. What I got was a time hack that I'll never forget. Instead of trying to do everything, pick just three. If three's not enough, combine areas that are important. For example, you don't have to give up time with your loved ones to keep up a great workout routine or run your business. You can work out with friends or even hire family you enjoy working with. I highly recommend involving kids if you have them.

As a business owner, it's all about working smarter until you experience the time freedom that comes once your fully operational and profitable. Seeing yourself through these periods of craziness can be difficult, but you've got to give yourself glimmers of hope to look forward to.

Become Self-Rewarding

The first time that I recognized my ability to reward myself for hard work or accomplishing something big was during the writing of my dissertation. No matter how much I wrote, I was never finished. Every time I submitted one more chapter for review, there were revisions requested before I could even begin to take a break.

During this time, I met a great man named Tim, and we started dating. I knew that I could never convince him that I couldn't hang out because I was too busy writing. This guy was seventeen years my senior. He wasn't going to go for the bull crap. What Tim showed me over the years was a work-for-reward process that has kept me sane and our relationship healthy.

Tim always liked to go out to dinner and showed me some great places to visit, but I had no time for fancy dinners. That was hours of time I would be liable for later. So, we decided to set two days a week that we could enjoy *date night* together. Date night has become kind of a joke in my family and network of friends because everyone knows that I do not deviate from date night. For eight years, I have chosen to get large projects completed by Wednesday and Saturday afternoons, that way Tim and I could enjoy going out to dinner or a movie on Wednesday and Saturday nights. The satisfaction that I feel by the time I make it out is incredible because I'm pushed to get things done by a certain day of the week. The next day is spent regrouping and gaining back momentum.

I challenge you to identify something that you love to do with your friends or loved ones. Put it as a reoccurring event on your schedule and commit to it.

Another reoccurring activity that is on my calendar is travel. The more you create wealth, the more you find that there are some incredible sites to see around the world, and I love seeing every single one of them. Four times a year, I book a vacation at my favorite resorts. Sometimes these trips are with my children, and other times these trips are adult trips that are for relaxation and regrouping. This is the gift to myself for working my butt off during that quarter. Likewise, my children find something great to look forward to with their mom when we have a trip scheduled together. Apparently, they don't mind riding my coattails down the money train so much.

Finding Friends Who Understand

It's incredibly hard to keep friendships with people who are no good for your business. They always know exactly how to make you want to hang up the phone or find the nearest exit. Mark Twain once said "Keep away from people who try to belittle your ambitions. Small people always do that, but the really great make you feel that you, too, can become great." That's because Mark Twain recognized that there are individuals who, out of their own insecurities or limitations, will try to diminish your dreams and aspirations. These people lack vision and the confidence to see beyond their own limitations and they'll project this negativity your way if you let them.

Find people who will motivate, inspire, and uplift you because they're out there. Find your tribe. These remarkable people will keep you grounded and will serve as a daily reminder of the path that you've committed to. When you find these people, cherish them and develop these relationships as they are the ones who truly understand the transformative power of encouragement and belief in our abilities.

Some People Are Simply Toxic

The first three years in business for me were filled with dozens of people, including family members, telling me that it was okay to close down if things didn't look like they were working out. I'd hear phrases like "don't let yourself get too deep in this," and "you know that most people can't afford to keep businesses going so always hold on to that day job." Like usual, I chalked it up to their lack of knowledge in the area of business ownership. But it's pretty hard to ignore negativity when it's constantly in your ear. We all know that one friend or family member who we are sure secretly wants to see us fold. That person is the exact reason that we've got to keep going and spend our time finding people who are supportive, resourceful, and creative.

As the years have gone by, it's become certain that I am only as good as the company I keep around me. These days, I only ask six- and seven-figure business owners for their input. They're the only ones who have the experience that I need to continue growing my business. There are friends who often have an opinion that they must share and yet can count their monthly sales on one hand. These aren't the people to go out to dinner with to small talk about your company. Find your network of people who outperform you, open up communication with them, and keep conversations with them routine.

SECTION IV
What Millionaires Do That You Should, Too

"When I started counting my blessings, my whole life turned around."

-Willie Nelson

Chapter 11
THE POWER OF AFFIRMATIONS, FAITH AND GRATITUDE

The greatest leaders, builders, athletes, business owners, and successful people all will tell you that their success is attributed to their own beliefs and abilities to get past previous failures. We'll talk about fear and failure very soon, but first let's focus on belief. We've all heard the hoopla of being able to achieve it if you can believe it, but it sure doesn't feel that way when there isn't enough money to cover the upcoming month's rent on our building. Believing in ourselves feels damn near impossible when a customer tells us that they hate our business policies, the necessary equipment for business stops working, or even worse, when the bank calls to tell us NO. These are the moments that hit business owners in the gut with a feeling of emptiness and worthlessness that none of our families or friends could possibly imagine.

One might call serial entrepreneurs or even brick-and-mortar business owners absolutely nuts. I mean, we dream up these crazy ideas until we see them flourish, all while putting out the fires of a business owner *and* dealing with our personal lives. I'd say that someone needs to call us freaking superheroes. But most days it just feels like people are throwing us problem after problem, and the moment that we catch up is the exact second that someone else needs our attention. It's hard not to feel overwhelmed or to question if this is even all worth the trouble.

Daily Affirmations

Do not let this be the section of the book that you skip because you don't believe in things such as meditation and affirmation. To be honest, I can't stand yoga because it personally drives me nuts. I can't meditate because I have probably developed later in life ADHD, or simply *monkey brain*. But the one thing that is a nonnegotiable in my day is reminding myself of who I am, what I believe, what I'm doing, and why I'm doing it. The moment you stop reminding yourself, life and other people will seize the opportunity to help you forget your passion, purpose, and plan. You may recall Muhammad Ali saying "I am the greatest. I said that even before I knew I was." That's because successful people know that they have to see themselves visually in their mind where they want to be before it can happen in real life. If you have not read Napoleon Hill's Think and Grow Rich or studied the power of thought, then let that be your next book read. Once you've read it, re-read it and allow your mind to work in your favor. You have to see your success before you experience it and this can be done through affirmations, meditation and visualization.

My daily affirmations are a set of principles that I believe, quotes that I have heard that have inspired me, or goals that I set for my particular business. They also include notes that I take when I am networking or working with leaders in my field. This list of affirmations includes actions that I need to complete each day, which I feel I need to be reminded of daily so that they become habitual. I update this list at least once every six months, and it is read ideally at the start of my day after a shower. That is my routine.

Create your own page of affirmations, reminders, and motivators based on quotes that have stuck with you or goals for the season that you're in. You can scribble them on Post-it Notes and put them around your work area or even type them out but reading them has to become routine.

My Daily Affirmations

I am brilliant. My mind is sculpted and created by God to deliver, to love, to inspire, to raise two brilliant men, to raise a brilliant company. Today I'm setting up my forever.

- My businesses have to be deemed and boasted as the best.

- It's not about being humble. WE ARE THE BEST!!!

- Money is expensive when you don't have it.

- Don't smile for no reason—give myself reasons to smile.

- Speak less. Speak clearly.

- It is okay to say NO every time that I want to.

- We make money with math and lose it with emotion.

- I will no longer be handicapped by my emotions.

- I am in love with my business. Today we're falling more in love.

- Master the processes of my business.

- I get paid first. Always.

- Money will come to me when I properly handle criticism.

- If you're not feeding me or fucking me, then I'm not interested in your opinion.

- How am I going to get a new client today?

- Check my SEO now.

- Check my bank accounts right away.

When Friends and Family Don't Understand

Friends and family who are not in business will barely respond to your comments about business ventures when you start out.
It doesn't mean they don't love you.
It's because you're going against all of their past beliefs.

They simply can't understand what you're doing.

Friends and family who see your business getting some pretty good traction will ask you frequently how things are going. Even if you're currently in the pits of hell, let them know things are going just fine,
because a person not in business
will quickly remind you that there are better employment options.

They simply can't understand what you're doing.

Friends and family who see your wild success will ask you, "How did you do it?" and "Who do you have helping you?" It's because they love money, too, but they simply can't understand what you're doing.

Just keep doing it.

Faith in Yourself and Self-Confidence

When people think about the word faith, they think that it's simply religious. It's not. The dictionary says it simply means to have complete trust or confidence in someone or something. I don't care what your spiritual or religious beliefs are, but the one person that you must grow faith in is yourself. Consistently remind yourself that you *are* already great and that you *can* reach your goal. So many people hustle their butts off. They have great ideas, great plans of execution, but they're missing the one ingredient of faith, which is fuel to getting this thing done. Have faith that the impossible can happen in your business and the self-confidence to get it done.

Having faith in the impossible is a crucial trait for any business owner. In the ever-evolving world of entrepreneurship, there will be countless challenges and obstacles that can seem insurmountable. However, it is precisely in these seemingly impossible situations that having faith becomes essential. Believing in the impossible will give you the courage and determination necessary to push through adversity, explore new solutions, and to take bold risks. It creates a mindset that embraces innovation, creativity, and unconventional solutions, to enable you to think beyond conventional boundaries and achieve extraordinary outcomes.

Faith in Your Team

There are times that I get so angry. I see emails going out with misspellings, sentences aren't properly formed, and when I ask them to proofread things for me, there are almost *always* errors. Sometime my staff don't word their statements exactly how I would to my customers, and their problem-solving is different than mine. While these might seem like small things, they drive a person like me absolutely nuts . . . enough to start talking to one of my mentors about it. It was during our conversation that I was reminded that I spent my career as a teacher. I have always held myself to standards of a professional working in a school, but I was paying nowhere near enough for me to expect my staff to have the same skill-sets and mannerisms. They are everyday people, working to pay their bills, and doing the two tasks that I asked them to do well—to get me new customers and to provide customer service that helps me keep my current customers.

If your team members are honorable, trustworthy, and meeting their basic responsibilities, then you have to trust them. Give them some authority and tools to lead. Trust your team.

Faith in your Network

Most business owners go from day to day living in a bubble. Hustle, hustle, hustle. If you're introverted like me, you might really be in trouble! While we're busy looking for the next customer or extinguishing fires caused by customers or lousy employees, we forget about the need to reach out to and spend adequate, well-structured time with people who have similar businesses and entrepreneurs who have different types of businesses than the ones that we run.

People ask me all the time if there is one thing that I recall taking me from an unprofitable business to a profitable one. Other than having a business coach, I would say that it was having an instantaneous network of people to reach out to on demand. People who knew my business, knew what I was going through, and offered solutions to come out of situations stronger and with more money in my pockets.

> **"Networking has been cited as the number one unwritten rule of success in business. Who you know really impacts what you know."**
>
> **-Sallie Krawcheck**

For many entrepreneurs, their idea of networking starts and ends at the local chamber of commerce meetings. Don't get me wrong, I *love* the chamber of commerce. Hell, they were complete strangers and the only ones who showed up to my ribbon-cutting. They tend to be great people. However, they are not always the most progressive groups of people who are innovative in growing their businesses.

Take advantage of online groups both on and off social media. Many of them have groups that are just for people in specific business fields. There isn't anything more amazing than having someone available who knows exactly what's happening in your life and can give you much more than the "I'm sure it'll all work out" that your family usually throws you. Sign up for conferences in your field and get to know people. These relationships are going to carry you through the hard times and often will end up being some of your best friendships.

Falling in Love with Your Company Again

The areas of our business that bring us the most problems tend to be the things that we start to avoid. It's not uncommon to want to walk away from your business for a period because of all the problem solving. There are three ways to get this issue out of the way so you can fall back in love with the business that you were and hopefully still are over the moon about. Write down the following:

a. What keeps taking up your time in the business?
b. Who keeps taking up your time in the business?
c. What do you prefer to be doing?

Now that you've identified those three, it's time to have a real conversation with yourself and hopefully a colleague. How can you fire those people or problems? Who can you put in your place to handle both a *and* b so that you can spend more time doing c? That is your task for the week and it's not optional. You've got to love the hell out of this business, because it's your baby.

The following task is a bit easier. Whether you have a commercial space or you work from home, you get to go shopping. Yes! Your second task is to pencil in going to one of your favorite stores to find one thing to purchase for your space that would make you love it even more. Something that just makes you feel good every time that you look at it. This idea came to me from a colleague named Alesya Burgio who owns a kick-ass company in Miami. After her recommendation, I came home and installed both the outside signage of my commercial building and a new aluminum sign inside. These were clearly high-end gifts to myself, but every time I see these two signs they signify both prestige and abundance. For those two items, I'll be forever grateful.

Gratitude

Practicing gratitude is essential for entrepreneurs as it brings numerous benefits to their personal and professional lives. Running a business can be demanding, and entrepreneurs often face challenges, setbacks, and stressful situations. Gratitude is crucial in keeping a positive mindset and perspective, allowing entrepreneurs to navigate these difficulties with resilience and optimism. You need each of these when navigating the rough waters of being an entrepreneur. Ultimately, practicing gratitude allows entrepreneurs to cultivate a mindset of abundance, resilience, and humility, leading to greater fulfillment, success, and well-being in both their personal and professional lives. This isn't to say that it's easy. Practicing gratitude when you're always busy putting out fires.

You've heard people call businesses ugly babies. Well, I've got news for you . . . the baby is yours! Okay, so you've got an ugly baby. It's okay. This same dream that you put together now keeps you up at night, always has something wrong with it, and needs your attention around the clock. That's okay too. We don't get this life at the cost of nothing. Sometimes, we pay in the form of brutal sacrifice to enjoy the life of an entrepreneur or at least to afford the ability to let out the wild animal of ideas stuck in our heads that won't ever calm down on their own. What we get in return can be ever sweet with the proper routines and procedures in place.

Instead of thinking about all the things that have the opportunity to frustrate you each day, take a moment to think about the things that you are able to do, either now that you have a business or now that you plan to have your business in full gear. Circle which ones you have or want and spend time each day being grateful for them. Many people would kill for this opportunity if they could figure out how to do it.

Things Business Owners Can Do that Others Can't

- Get out of bed when you choose

- Work in your pajamas if you choose

- Control your own job description

- Flexible work hours

- Spending more time with family

- Availability to see your family off each day

- Time for travel that a job doesn't provide

- The profits go to you

- You don't have to constantly impress a boss

- You don't need to answer to anyone

- No more long commutes

- Saving gas from not having the long commutes

- Open-ended career progression

- Satisfaction of hiring/supporting employees and their families

- Creating a business based on your values

- No one to fire you

- The ability to retire sooner

- The ability to save more for retirement than a traditional 401K allows

- The ability to pass on a business to a loved one if you choose

Our daily routines are up to us.

If there is something on this list you can't do yet, put the people and planning in place to make it happen!

Chapter 12
LIVING FEARLESSLY

I did it. I told my boss that I would be resigning from my job. Earlier in the book, I told you about how great it felt to tell them to kiss my grits, but I didn't tell you that the sweat was dripping down the middle of my back as I thought about the fact that I only had a little over $400 in my personal account at the moment. But it was too late. The words already came out my mouth. I couldn't take them back. She said, "Wow. This is huge. I would never have expected this. Are you sure?" And I lied my ass off. I mean I deserve a freaking Emmy. I excitedly told her that I was certain, and I was looking forward to investing all my time into the wonderful business I created.

Like I said, it was all lies. I had no idea what was ahead. The only thing I knew was that I was full *in it* now, and that the weight of the world was off my shoulders. The cats out of the bag. If my kids are going to eat, it's now going to be because I will work my butt off and make my business work for me.

It makes perfect sense to me that only 6 percent of adults actually own a business. I bet that at least 30 to 40 percent actually want to own a business but they're missing the guts and filled with fear. But fear can't be in the equation when you run a business. It can be sensed just as quickly as a shark smells blood in the water. Fear is absolutely crippling and will keep you from growing to anywhere close to your potential. If nothing else, fear alone can take down your business.

Fear of Failing Friends and Family

Family can really be a funny thing. Family members show their love and support for us in various ways, but most of all through their routinely scheduled questions, "So how's everything going? Are you making sure that you're not going in the red?" Bless their hearts, they truly mean well. They're just completely lost when it comes to running a business. We already talked about being prepared with your go-to statements when they ask you how things are going. But more importantly, remember that you owe no one anything. The only person you need to prove things to is yourself. As a result, your family will get to reap the benefits.

Fear of Not Having Enough Money

Less than 8% of adults are self-employed. That means the rest of them are employed by someone like you. This has to be because of society's need for stability, security, a lack for resources to start a business, or the average person's desire to avoid risks. There's a multitude of rational reasons to avoid going into business for.

If I had to take a crack at the number one fear business owners have, I'd guess it's not having enough money to pay their bills. Rent, utilities, payroll, insurance, taxes. All of this weighs so heavily on us at nighttime and what happens is that we end up spending so much time worrying about it that we don't focus on bringing in new money.

Taking massive action is of paramount importance for entrepreneurs. In the fiercely competitive business world, mere ideas and intentions are not enough to create success. It is through relentless and decisive action that entrepreneurs can turn their visions into reality. Taking massive action means going above and beyond the norm, challenging the status quo, and pushing the limits of what is deemed possible. Take massive levels of action is the only one way to rid yourself of the feeling of going broke and not having enough. You must actively market. Actively promote yourself and your business. Actively put out new advertisement campaigns. Actively determine which marketing campaigns can put money in your pocket, even if it means collecting payments up front so you don't have to wait on the cash. Actively seeking money from banks, investors, or even family and friends.

Most of all, keep records of successful actions you take so that you will remember them in the future because money will always be needed in business. Sometimes it's just easier to find than other times. Keeping records of these successful actions will allow you to leverage your own experience and expertise, building on previous triumphs and avoiding past mistakes. By documenting successful strategies, processes, and approaches, you can create a valuable repository of knowledge that can be tapped into for future decision-making. These records serve as a reference point, providing insights into what has worked effectively in the past and enabling you to replicate those successes.

One sure way to fail and go broke is to stop being active and turn attention away from the processes within the business that keeps money flowing inward.

Fear of Competitors

When I first opened my business, I was scared to death. I signed my lease and was now stuck with a property that I only hoped would turn out to be amazing. I signed the lease, got the keys from the realtor, and jumped in my car to go check out my office space for the first time alone.

As I drove down the street, I passed a competitor who I knew was right down the street from me. An ache filled my stomach as I drove by because I knew they were the only music school in town, and they were huge. They had all the customers, and I feared that I'd never get my share. As I passed another few blocks, I couldn't believe it! They were hanging up a freaking sign to open another music school within blocks of me! Why in the world would we need three music schools all within blocks of each other? This was insane. I hadn't even gotten into my building yet. Surely, one of us wouldn't be here in a year's time.

Over my first two years in business, I would spend a great deal of time worrying about my competitors. How much were they charging? Were some of our clients leaving and going to them? I was completely consumed. We would mystery shop them and get all the information that we could. We did this for years until one day my office manager said, "Dr. T, this is pathetic. We keep calling these places, but they suck! We have more students, and all of our students who register say they're so glad that they came to us and quit the others."

It was at that moment that I realized we weren't just as good, we were better. On that day, I stopped being afraid of my competitors. We even started referring business to them for services we didn't offer.

One day I decided to break our unwritten code of silence, and I called the newer competitor and asked him if we could swap brochures. He was ecstatic. I went over to give him our materials, and he informed me that he doesn't even teach music at the store anymore because we took all the customers in the area. Now he just sells and rents instruments. This was perfect! Our businesses could now cross-market to each other! Ever since that day, I bring doughnuts and bagels to them with our brochures and gladly accept theirs as friends in commerce.

The other music school that already had the town's customers *locked down* was a different story. We kept our distance until one day, we called to ask if they sold a tool that we needed to fix a drum set. He told us that he didn't but since we were always so kind sending them customers, he would deliver us his personal tool from home to get it fixed. Go figure! Bottom line, your competitors are not your enemies. You can only be your own enemy. Make friends in the community, market your ass off, and then *crush them*—with a smile, of course.

Chapter 13
THE POWER OF PERSEVERANCE

I'd like to share my background story of how I learned the skills necessary to build a successful company. It began in my high school years. I loved school. Had great friends, cute boyfriends, excelled in sports, had lead roles in drama productions. You name it, I did it. That was until a hot September morning during our soccer warm-ups. I kept throwing up. Every quarter of a mile or so, it kept happening. This wasn't like me. I'm *awesome* at running. To this day, I can give you my half marathon without vomiting.

I knew something had to be wrong.

I left soccer practice and headed to the local pharmacy where I secretly tried to hide the pregnancy test that I was holding. I busted the box open as soon as I got home. And there it was. My future was shattered by two bright lines. I was sixteen and pregnant.

I hid it from my family for about two months until I had to come out with it. To date, my junior year of high school was my most difficult year ever. Not just because of the shame I had brought upon myself and my family, but because I worked my ass off that year. I networked with other pregnant students to find out how they got by. I worked two jobs and showed up to school every day. Even when I couldn't fit in the school desks anymore, I would sit on the windowsill of the classroom.

My soccer and track coaches said that I couldn't participate in sports because it was a liability, but my music teacher still allowed me to actively participate in our activities. I stayed in the game and worked harder than most kids.

My bouncing baby boy Malachi was born April 26. The funny thing is, even having a baby doesn't get you out of classes. The school sent a tutor to the hospital for my lessons the day after I had a C-section, and she continued to work with me at home for six weeks. Soon I realized that real life wasn't going to stop for me. This was especially evident five days after I had my son. I was scheduled to take my SATs. Like every other day, I showed up. In pain from surgery and in agony from hours going by without nursing my newborn, I tore my way through every question on the examination, then I ran out after finishing my last question and knew at that moment, things would never be the same.

I knew I would have to work harder than everyone else.

As I entered my senior year, things got a little better. I doubled up on classes and was able to graduate a semester early with honors. The awards were coming in from everywhere. My athletics department, the music department, hell, I even got the Superintendent's Award. Graduating early gave me the opportunity to start college a little early. Two years were spent at a community college, and I decided to transfer to my dream school. I always considered being a music teacher, so I applied to the Crane School of Music four hours away from home. Somehow, I got accepted and off to college I went. Just my three-year-old son and me.

College Life

I thank God every day for my opportunity to go off to college. But like everything in my life, it didn't exactly turn out as I expected. I rented an awesome three-bedroom, fully furnished house. I had saved up more than $3,000 to last me through the first few months of school in a rural upstate town in New York. Everything was super cheap in this area, but I knew the money wouldn't last too long. I'd figured that I'd get a job at some point, but I was good to go for the meantime. I held onto my money and kept it with me wherever I went, especially because my new landlord informed me that the lock on my back door was going to need fixing.

My family drove me up in the U-Haul to our new home. As they finished getting me settled in and left with the U-Haul, I remember this awesome feeling of excitement for a new chapter beginning, but also fear of being left in a new place. It was just going to be me and a three-year-old. I felt all by myself. I was in a little tiny town called Potsdam, New York. Even my cell phone didn't have service up there. I wouldn't be able to reach anyone until my landline got installed a week later. I had arrived in Potsdam four days before school was scheduled to begin. The first few days were spent just unpacking, but it was quiet. I mean *real* quiet. Not much human contact, no cable, no phone. I would go to the local gas station to use the pay phone to check in with my family.

The Friday before school opened, I jumped in my car and headed back to the gas station to call my mom. She was so excited to hear that things were going well. I hung up the phone with a smile and headed into the convenient store to buy some snacks. The clerk was nice enough, and I remember thinking, "*I can't believe people are so nice here.*"

After the clerk rang me up, I turned around and the life just melted out of me. I couldn't believe it. There was someone reaching inside my car. The moment I took a step forward, they sped off in their car. I ran outside and couldn't believe it. I had left my window down with all my money in the car. It was still in cash because my bank wasn't in that town, and I hadn't even opened an account yet—$3,860 gone *just like that.*

I was crushed. "What am I supposed to do?" I asked myself. I was in a new town completely alone with not even enough change to use the pay phone again. How could I pay rent? How would I afford daycare on Monday? How would we eat? I called my mom back collect this time with tears in my voice, and she saved the day . . . well, actually a few weeks. But I knew this would be only short-lived. I had to make money.

The following day, I started looking for ways to make money online, and I began selling items I had through Craigslist. I would find little jobs that I could do from home between school hours and was even blessed with good fortune when my university's childcare called to say that they had a spot for my son while I was in classes and they would charge me a whopping $2.31 per week because it was subsidized. I just needed to keep my grades good. Again, $2.31 per week.

I think I can handle this.

My remaining years in Potsdam weren't easy but they were joyful. I was broke and on food stamps, so I had to hustle. When it came time to renew my lease, I realized that I couldn't afford to stay in the house I was renting. My little boy and I were going to have to move into a little apartment closer to my school. But when I left the house, I lost more than just the space. I lost all our furniture. I slept on my living room floor for the six months before I graduated. The only reason that I bought blinds for my living room was so that my classmates wouldn't walk past my apartment and laugh at me sleeping on the hard living room floor.

The grind never stopped, and I kept envisioning my next step in life. I wanted to move to New York City to pursue my music, teaching, and the boyfriend whom I had been having a long-distance relationship with for the past two years. I would visualize myself living in New York City no matter how crazy my friends and family thought I was. The semester before I graduated, I even packed up all our items in the house. Everything was put into boxes that said "NYC." They filled my bedless bedroom, but it was okay. I was working to fulfill a dream.

Ridgewood, Queens

I did it! Another U-Haul trip with my family. This time it was to New York City. It was two days before Christmas, and I was moving into a tiny railroad style apartment that I had never seen before moving day. My boyfriend who lived in Queens had picked it out for me, and I was so excited to be in the city that never sleeps.

The only problem was that it wasn't just the city that wasn't sleeping. I wasn't either. I didn't do too good of a job preparing to live in the city. My rent had gone from $500 per month to $1,100 per month. I found a high school that was going to allow me to complete my required internship for graduation, but it was an hour commute from home. The wonderful daycare I had found before I moved to New York City had shut down, and I was left with no clue about who would watch my son, who was now almost ready for kindergarten. I was stressed out every day, gaining tons of weight from not eating the right food, and was even hospitalized multiple times for stress-induced illnesses. To make matters worse, I found out that my boyfriend of three years had been cheating on me since I met him.

The little perfect apartment that he found for me across town from him was strategically located so I would never see his girlfriend, who was living with him and his mother.

Things were just *not* working out.

It was then that I learned I had to use what I had to get back on my feet. I searched online for daycares and found a young woman who was six months pregnant and looking to make some extra money. She took great care of my son while I was working and became a longtime friend. I would get up early in the mornings to go for a run since I couldn't afford a gym membership anymore. Sadly, I'd even use those runs to pick up loose change on the ground. Best of all, I remembered that I had a skill. I was almost a certified music teacher, a great musician, and a damn good voice teacher. I converted my living room into a teaching space and started charging the highest that I could get people to pay me, which was $80 an hour. The rest was history.

That year, I did unspeakable things to try and pay rent. I ended up breaking my lease early to find a better home on Long Island where my son could attend a good school. I'd found a full-time job teaching and a nicer space to invite my private clients.

As I began unpacking and decorating my new home in Glen Cove, Long Island, I hung my awards from school. There was one that was in a box that I'd never even opened. It was the Superintendent's Award from high school. I couldn't believe that I'd never read the inscription. It said *Superintendent's Award for Perseverance*. Perseverance. Wow. It was a concept I had never thought about. All I could equate the last five years of my life to was struggle. What I didn't realize was that struggling and failing were so important in my *process*. Struggle was the reason I had a kid two weeks after my seventeenth birthday and *still* graduated from my dream college on time. It was the reason I was able to make my skills work for me through entrepreneurship. It's the only way I got through my doctorate degree at age twenty-seven while teaching full time and having another toddler.

Resourcefulness, faith in ourselves, and the ability to lead fearlessly in your businesses are keys to success but the real secret to creating a wonderful, profitable business is the power of perseverance. When the cash runs out and the problems start piling on, it's going to be your *will* to continue grinding despite everything going wrong that will see you through. Don't give up on a dream. Just wake up, grind, learn something new, be better than you were yesterday, and repeat.

SECTION V
When It All Goes Wrong

Chapter 14
SCREW THE BUSINESS PLAN

When I told a friend the title of this book, he laughed and said it reminded him of the character named Lawrence from a show called *Insecure*. Lawrence had lost his job and was on the couch for six months working on his business plan. Meanwhile, his girlfriend was supporting them and getting pretty tired of hearing about this so-called *business plan*. What she needed was to see some action. Some sales. Something to keep her remotely interested.

While my friend and I laughed about this exact scenario, it really hit home with me. That literally *was* the story of how my business started, failed, failed again, and then grew to wild success.

I formed my business when I was twenty-one years old and fresh out of college. I was unemployed and lucky enough to have an ambitious best friend who was extremely successful and driven to get her business going. I spent my unemployed days at home filing paperwork for the company, designing cool letterheads, and launching a company, going back and forth to my best friend for feedback because after all, at least her business was getting some checks.

I opened a business account with Staples and bought a turbo-printer to print out pamphlets for a kid's summer camp that would never enroll a single kid. Best of all, I had the most detailed business plan that one could create. It took months to perfect my plan. Months went by, and I got a few clients here and there. I got offered a great job, and my business took a seat on the sideline. It took five years for me to decide that I actually had enough money to open up a building for my business and that I was willing to give up all my time to make it work, even though I still had my full-time job as a public school teacher. Five years. The months leading up to me opening my business's doors were spent deep in my business plan, counting the numbers, checking out how other similar businesses were making their money and how I could make plenty of it. My plan was perfect! PERFECT.

My platform in the community gave me access to the clients that I needed. I found the perfect building with rent I could afford. My good friend was willing to work for cheap to help me get the business growing while I was at work, and there was plenty of money in my bank account so that I could have every opportunity to succeed. Open the doors and here we go!

I had no clue. No freaking clue at all.

Employees Won't Care As Much As You Do

When you first open the doors to your business, you spend time choosing people to work for you who you think will be a really a great fit for your company. People who work for you in the beginning either have nothing to lose, or have a lot of faith in you because it takes a lot of guts to take a job from someone who hasn't been writing payroll checks consistently. These people opened and closed my doors every day and delivered pretty good service to our clients. But there would be many days when conversations weren't worded the way I thought they should be to customers. The upkeep of the building was rearranged according to the desires of the staff and not what I envisioned for *my* building. And the teachers who worked for me . . . God bless their hearts, they had no flipping clue how to treat my customers the way that I wanted.

The first year was often spent wondering, "Why the heck don't they already know this stuff?" It took another five years to figure out that not everyone was me. And while I've since trained my staff to think more like me, they can't read my mind, and I've got to know that they aren't losing sleep tonight if sales go down. They didn't dream this thing up, save up their money for it, and get the knots in their stomachs leading up to opening day in fear of not getting the first customer. No one will care for your business, your baby, the way that you do.

Tracy's Story

"I've had so many moments that were totally unexpected. There are so many things that you can't plan for. There's just no planning. But being in business, I often think about the interoffice romance that happened with my office manager and one of my instructors at my music school.

It was a friend and colleague of the guitarist at my studio, and I knew his wife. Well, one day his wife called me and said, "I need to talk to you. Will you be there today?" I said, "Sure, I'll be there by 2:00 p.m." So, I met her there, we went inside, and she said, "I hate to be the person to tell you this, but my husband and your office manager are doing more than conducting music lessons here at the studio." And me and my mind honestly thought they were stealing paper or making copies, printing out flyers that they shouldn't be or something like that!

Little did I know that they had been meeting there, before students arrived obviously, and they were getting busy! They were doing their thing at the studio. This was before I had security cameras up. I was oblivious to what was going on for apparently several weeks. I was clueless. They would just come in and do their thing! How everything came to light was that the instructor started feeling super guilty and confessed everything to his wife. So it got really weird after that. I was livid.

I went full CSI. I went to Walmart and got a pet-stain kit with a blue light and the glasses. I'm going around the studio looking for fluids. I didn't know what else to do! Fortunately, I didn't find anything. Meanwhile, the guitar instructor was so wrapped up with guilt. He literally resigned from guilt, but he had some other issues going on like substance abuse and ended up being Baker-Acted. He spent some time in the hospital, and it was just a mess! The office manager resigned before I could boot her. She got out of there! Thankfully it was invisible to the customers. That was the saving grace but it was a mess for a hot minute! -Tracy Morris, Morris Music Academy

More Money, More Problems

There aren't too many things other than taxes and death that are certain in life. However, one thing I know for sure is that you don't have a business if you don't have problems. It's inevitable and yet so important if you want a profitable business. Some problems will be as small as a bad review on Yelp from a competitor, a little bigger like catching your staff in all sorts of acts within your company, or even your building burning down. A wise man told me, "If you ain't got problems, you don't have a business," and that is so true. We are problem solvers on a daily basis. The good news is that there are two things you can do that will help you become wildly successful in your business.

1. Prepare for common problems
2. Turn off your emotions and think strategically

People Won't Understand

We started to talk about family sabotage in the last chapter (bless their hearts), but I've come to learn that no one in my life would understand what I was doing, why I would make these insane sacrifices of my time or money to do it, and that most people thought without a doubt that my business would fail. They would never tell me that I would fail, they were far too polite for that (even though that's what they meant).

Every time I visited my parents or declined an invitation to another lame-ass party, I was met with mumbles of disbelief and confusion. If I had my laptop open, my mom would ask me, "Do you have more homework to complete?" Mind you, I'm thirty-four years old. I finished my PhD seven years ago, haven't taken a class in years, and my mother is 100 percent still in her right mind. Okay? This is what we're dealing with. No mom, I *don't* have homework. What I have is payroll coming up due soon, marketing emails that need to go out within an hour, and six days left to find staff to replace someone who quit last week without notice.

Geez, all this damn pressure. People won't understand. Hell, I don't understand! Although I was handicapped from getting things off the ground for a long time, the first ten years after I formed my business were spent working as a public school teacher. By year eleven as a teacher, my business was ridiculously successful and out of control. My teaching income was six-figures. So yeah, why would I need to work day and night on a business that I didn't need? Well, the answer is because I'm wired that way. We're entrepreneurs, and we can't get through breakfast without thinking about our next project or big idea. That's the demon that we face every day. It doesn't require a $600 per hour psychiatrist, but it does require that you become "okay" with people not understanding what you do, especially when you are in your first decade of running your business and still trying to perfect your systems.

This problem can seriously destroy families and relationships.

- Focus on finding balance for time with your loved ones.

- Find comfort in knowing that your hard work will be worth it over time.

Plan for People to Want Things Free or Cheap

My sons Malachi and Julien have expensive tastes. What can I say, they are money-grubbing pains in the ass when they want to be. Their friends seem to have all the latest gadgets and overpriced clothing. I guess everyone in town apparently has a ton of money to spare on their kids. Who woulda thought? When the boys come to me telling me their rationale for needing the latest iPhone or asking for Xbox gift cards that they just intend to spend to purchase fake money on Grand Theft Auto, I'm the one who either has to shut them down or cough it up. No one chimes in to say, "Talonda, I'm gonna throw you some money to cut down on the expense of raising your kids or giving in to their occasional desires." Yet, what I receive often from friends is the request to lower *my* prices for *them*.

My friend Dee has a great government job. Her husband does pretty well for himself, too. When I first opened my business, Dee called me to have a conversation that would stick with me for years. "Talonda, I'm so glad that your music school is doing so great. My kids love lessons, and we want to add two more lessons—piano for my youngest and a voice class for my daughter Grace. We really can't afford to pay for the additional lessons. If I add two and pay for the extra one, maybe you can help me out?" I was only a few months into running my business and barely had any customers, so I needed every client that I could get. Why the hell wouldn't I be thinking about counting dollars instead of counting heads in the building?

That first year, I gave discounts to about forty people. My other twenty clients paid the lowest prices in town because I assumed that low prices would bring more customers. What I have ended up stuck with is a group of poorly behaved and entitled customers who have been grandfathered in at prices up to 80 percent lower than my newer clients. They are completely okay with killing my bottom line and really would steal a kidney from my nine-year-old if I allowed them. The vultures will see you doing well and don't care about your bills. Do not discount. Ever.

Lessons Learned

I'll never forget the day my seventeen-year-old caught me in the driveway. I was wiped out. An employee had just put in their resignation at the office, I completely had forgotten an appointment that I had scheduled, and there were 500 report cards I needed to grade for my day job. As I approached the house, my son met me before the steps to remind me that I had forgotten about his little brother's concert that night and had double booked myself because I also had forgotten that he wanted a ride to one of his football practices. In desperation, I told him, "I screwed up. I'm a sucky mom today. And it won't be the only day either." I simply had too much going on and wasn't organizing my schedule well that week.

> *There aren't too many things that I can promise. But I can tell you for certain that I've screwed up a lot and will screw up a thousand times more.*

You see, I'm what I'd call a self-proclaimed overachiever. I wake up early and go to bed late when there's work to be done. I think through decisions and plan quite meticulously. But I learned with every passing day that all my great planning and organizational qualities meant diddly-squat when first learning how to run my business. Some of it was going to come from trial and error. And a whole lot of error.

The first years, I made a series of terrible mistakes. Each one of them could have been catastrophic enough to make me close my business, but my perseverance got me through. I would like to share with you some of my memorable mistakes in the hope that you'll avoid them.

Cutting Corners

Thanksgiving is a wonderful time of year. We're not quite at Christmas but the feeling of togetherness and crisp air begin to remind me of time spent with family. At least that was the feeling that I had two months after opening my business. We're a kid's business so I naturally opened up at the start of the school year. On top of that, I managed to actually have some customers by Thanksgiving time. It was awesome! For the holidays, I decided to travel to my parent's beautiful upstate home three hours north of Long Island. I was able to relax, regroup, and let my family know how successful things were turning out for me in the big city.

After a four-day weekend, I traveled home and made sure to arrive in the afternoon so that I had the opportunity to check on things at the office before we reopened the Monday after Thanksgiving. I dropped off my kids at home and drove to my business. The moment I opened the door, something didn't sound right. I took a step and there is it was. My worst nightmare. Water.

There was water everywhere! I ran back toward the single bathroom in the building to see where the water was coming from, but it just kept flowing. Not only the water but also supplies and important papers. Instruments such as guitars and pianos were completely submerged in water. My first reaction was to look for towels. Yes, towels! What the heck would towels do? We didn't have a single towel in our office. It was eight o'clock on a Sunday night, and I couldn't think of a single store nearby with *towels*. My family and friends lived hours away, and that was the first moment that I realized I was completely alone in this. All I could do as the tears flowed down my face was call the landlord. Thank God he lived nearby. He raced over, shut off the water, and busted out the water vacuum.

We stayed well into the middle of the night trying to remove water. I think that the desperation in my face let him know that I was physically and emotionally worn out, so he sent me home and told me he'd talk to the insurance company in the morning.

On the way home, all I could think of was, "What did I do wrong? And what type of faulty property did I just sign a five-year lease for?" It was that moment that I realized that I had turned down the heat to fifty-eight degrees before I left to head out of town. Who would have known we'd have a sudden drop in temperature? Why the heck wouldn't I have left water dripping and the temperature up while we were closed? The answer is because I was an inexperienced twenty-something-year-old who didn't know how pipes burst.

Somehow a miracle happened the next day, the landlord informed me that the insurance would take care of this but even better, he'd have his workers in there tearing out walls and getting things fixed quickly. Since we had just opened, we weren't expecting clients in the office until Thursday at 3:00 p.m., and the construction workers got everything completed by Thursday at 2:45 p.m. Just in the nick of time. Our heat now remains on seventy degrees, twenty-four hours a day. As a result, our utility bill has actually decreased.

Lesson learned: I don't cut corners to save money. It can be costly.

Taking Recommendations from the Wrong People

When I was ready to start making some sales, I knew that I had to get an accountant. My dad had always done my taxes, but he hadn't ever done a business tax return. I decided to check out a few accountants. First, I called one of the moms from my son's football team who I knew had a business. I asked her if she had an accountant she could recommend to me, and she hastily rushed me off the phone responding with, "I don't know anyone." She clearly didn't want to share with me the person who handles her books. I guess the rumors of her family being associated with the mob might be true after all. I know they keep things *in house*.

After that failed attempt for a recommendation, I got on Google and searched for a great accountant in the area. I went to their fancy office in a very affluent section of Long Island, and I just *knew* that they must know what they were doing. They had me pay about $300 to file a few papers that I didn't quite understand so I could start doing business and then informed me that they would charge $1,500 to file my return each year. Holy crap! Apparently, I'd be paying for that fancy knowledge of theirs.

The first year, I reported a big loss. After all, we were a new business. The second year, we reported another loss but it wasn't too bad. These refunds were actually pretty great. The next year we were really making money and sure enough, I owed Uncle Sam. Jerk. I paid the bill and kept it moving, but then suddenly, I started receiving notices from the state that I owed them money and that there was an error in how my business was set up. The notices also said that I owed back corporate taxes.

I don't understand. I'm a sole proprietor. I wasn't an S Corp or anything like that. So, I reached out to my amazing accountant, and he told me he'd make a call and not to sweat it. So, no sweat was coming down my forehead. It wasn't until one September day that I received a final notice from the state that they were about to garnish any funds that we received when processing credit cards from our customers. What the heck? "How is this possible?" I screamed while trying to catch my breath. How would I even make payroll if our income gets garnished?

I frantically called my accountant, whose secretary informed me *as usual* that he wasn't available and would get back to me. One call. Two calls. Three emails—nothing. That's when I quickly called one of my friends in the area who had a lucrative kids' business just like mine.

He gave me his accountant's contact information, and I called him quickly to schedule a meeting.

After making the one-hour trip to this accountant, I sat down and showed him all our filings and notices from the state. That was the moment that I knew I was in trouble. He informed me that the original accountant that I met one time at the fancy office had created a corporation for me in error. In addition, the small problem that my awesome accountant said was no big deal turned out to be a very big deal.

All of a sudden, I was met with thousands of dollars that I owed. I had to file five years' worth of back corporate tax returns and late penalties, all because I took the word of an accountant who was recommended by someone whom I love, but who had not seen this accountant's experience filing for an actual company like mine. The result was quite expensive, but it could have been worse if I didn't have the money to foot the bill at the time. The government could have forcibly taken the money they estimated that I owed them due to this error, and thirty people could have been left with paychecks that bounced.

Lesson learned: Make sure that all my vendors are vetted and highly recommended by other profitable people in my business area.

Hiring Too Fast

They say, "hire slow and fire fast," but it's hard to do this in real life if you let yourself get desperate. My company is open twelve hours a day, seven days a week. While I was working my full-time job, I had to rely on full-time staff to hold down the fort at my business. In the process of hiring, I've found some great people, most of the time in quite unorthodox ways.

My first receptionist was a very close friend of mine. She was wonderful and stayed more than a year, which was great since her goal was just to stay long enough to get me rolling. My next receptionist was a crazy elderly woman, and I was fine with that experience. But it was the 2017 year that blew me away. I had managed to hire and fire ten people for the same position. One after the next, after the next, after the next. None of them were right for the position, and the only thing in common between them was that I had hired them. Each of them I had thought was perfect for the position simply because I quickly needed someone in there. One girl quit after two weeks because she thought the job was too much work, and another beat her record, lasting only thirty-six hours!

As a travel-loving boss, I got the phone call while I was out of the county that the woman hadn't shown up to work and was quitting on day two because she was hoping not to do anything other than answer phones. It was at that moment that I realized that I had been hiring too fast. No matter how great I thought these people were, I didn't take my time to see all the candidates who could have possibly been better. But even though hiring fast was a big issue, I've learned that firing slow is even worse.

Charity was originally hired to be my personal assistant, but we ended up tweaking her position to Director of Special Projects. Meaning, she was supposed to make sure all our projects and events were well planned and awesome. She was great at it, until she showed up to one of our events. The students of my music school had our second performance of the winter season at Carnegie

Hall. Charity showed up but wouldn't speak to anyone. At the end of the show, she walked onto the stage with the performers who were dressed in their full ball gowns and tuxedos to photo-bomb their beautiful picture commanding the stage while wearing jeans, a T-shirt, and sketchers. This was the first day of red flags that something was wrong. The next day there were errors in Charity's work, so she was written up for not following policy. All of a sudden, she didn't feel well and needed to go home sick. Red flag number three.

At this point, I should have been looking to replace Charity, and I was. But she beat me to it. She wrote her letter of resignation on a piece of paper and said that February 15 would be her last day. I'll never forget the date because Charity spent the following thirteen days refusing to do work. Every request from her supervisor to get something done was followed up with, "I'm busy, can't you do it?" It was incredible.

The final straw was on Valentine's Day. A staff member sent me an SOS message that Charity had kids crying in the lobby because she was telling everyone that tomorrow was her last day and that I didn't respect her. She was smearing my name and the reputation of my company while I was eating Chicken Madeira in my favorite restaurant. I let her stay so that I could have someone else doing the work while I relaxed with a glass of wine and chicken, for crying out loud!

That was it. I had to cut my Valentine's Day dinner short to tell her not to come in for her last day of work. Charity should have been paid out to leave when she put in her notice and not given time to infiltrate my customer base, causing me to do damage control.

Lesson learned: Hire very slow and always have a backup choice for new hires. Fire fast and never let a problem employee stay during their two-week notice if they are going to do damage. Speak to your attorney and work out a way to pay them through that time period.

Surveillance

The second year in business, I told my mentor that I felt stuck. He told that I needed cameras to check out what was going on in my building while I wasn't there. So, like a good little schoolgirl, I followed through and got one nice camera.

There are so many things that new business owners forget to do or simply don't know how to do when they first open. Even though I have a children's business, it never dawned on me to put security cameras in every room until I found out some other music schools had them put in.

I had eight rooms at the time but could only afford one camera, so I put it above the people who were responsible for making our sales at the front desk. Over the first month, it was pretty boring stuff. Paper filing, phone calls, the occasional texting offenders, etc. This was especially true for my daytime worker who hated cleaning. She especially hated mopping, vacuuming, or tidying up the lobby. But come on, cleaning and people sitting at a desk? Who wants to watch that all day? Well, one day on my lunch break at work, I decided to call the receptionist to see how things were going. Ring, ring, ring. This went on for more than a minute. Hmmm. I could've sworn she was supposed to be at work.

Okay. I'm pissed! I'm paying her to answer the damn phone so we can get customers. Why isn't she picking up? She better be signing up a client on the other line! I decided to go back to surfing the net, then jumped up and yelled, "WAIT! I forgot about the cameras!" I pulled up the screen, and I swear the camera feed came in clearer than the high-def televisions at Best Buy. The first thing that struck me was my office staff's mopping technique. She was spraying the floor with Windex and using paper towels under her feet to wipe it dry. Again, she was *spraying* the floor with *Windex* and using *paper towels underneath her feet* to wipe it dry. It gets better. After the floors were done being *mopped,* she went on to vacuuming.

This worker grabbed the vacuum, but it didn't look like she was setting it up to begin vacuuming. It looked like she was taking it apart and getting ready to relax. What the hell!? It was at that moment that things quickly turned, and I realized what was happening. There she was in all her glory. My receptionist. Legs spread eagle, her head back and mouth open in great pleasure while pleasing herself with my vacuum cleaner! Who would even think of using the vacuum special add-on parts for those purposes? My camera footage could have competed against any Stormy Daniels late-night special.

At least she finally picked up the vacuum.

That view was not something that I had included in my business plan, but it was the first time I realized that I needed a plan for how to deal with uncomfortable situations like that. I mean, what do you say to a person when that happens? Most of all, why didn't I think of having an employee handbook that would make it easy to fire people for masturbation in the office? Looks like a good time to hire a labor law attorney because, believe me, this isn't the craziest thing you'll see on camera.

Lesson learned: Cameras are not optional. You will not believe what you see sometimes. Also, removable vacuum parts are interchangeable. That is all.

Forty Cents on the Dollar

Business owners are no strangers to shimmying and shaking to get needed money. For me, it was the realization that the month of May was going to have an extra cycle of payroll that I had not planned for. Who had an extra twenty grand lying around for that? Not me.

Luckily, I took out a loan more than a year ago when we expanded. I was very fortunate. They gave me $50,000 to build out our location, and the interest wasn't too bad. The company simply deducted monthly payments out of my account. As a result, we were able to grow!

Every six months, the loan company would ask me if I'd like to refinance and get more cash. I mean, who couldn't use more cash for marketing or in my case, payroll? So, I of course took the loan. At this point, the loan was up to $130,000. I never imagined that I'd need that much for a loan for my business, but I took out enough to cover six months of loan payments and hoped that I would have the extra cash available to pay it off sometime that year.

Since I'm such a planner, I thought it would be a great idea to run a plan past my business coach. He told me about American Express's loan programs for merchants and how it works out great for him. When he asked me how much my interest was, I told him it was *about* 10 percent. "Ten percent!" he yelled. "That's crazy!"

Wow. I hadn't thought about that. I actually thought I was one of the lucky ones who got a loan. Well, since I was hesitant and wasn't quick enough to identify how much my interest rate was, I decided to take a quick peek at my loan contract. I pulled it up on my computer, and I couldn't believe my eyes. Forty percent. Forty. Freaking. Percent.

How could I have done this? How could I quickly renew a loan without realizing that the interest rate was 40 percent? I called the loan company, and they informed me that my first loan was at 10 percent interest but this higher loan was at the increased interest rate. This mistake would literally cost me $580.43 cents in payments per day for an entire year. It spoke volumes. Inundated with everything else around me and so quickly excited by money, I could have easily signed my life away.

Lesson learned: Read the fine print every time, even if it's a company that I've done business with previously.

The Sixty-four Dollar Client

When I graduated college with a degree in music education, I knew that I wanted to be involved with vocal coaching. What could be better than teaching people how to sing? So, I moved myself right to New York City and set up a teaching area in my overpriced railroad style apartment. Out of the gate, I set a price of eighty dollars an hour. Yes, this twenty-one-year-old girl with zero experience had the *audacity* to tell people to their faces that they would need to pay me eighty bucks an hour. And they did. All I needed was the balls to ask for it.

For some reason, this bravery went out the window the moment that I opened my business. I wanted my prices to be the best in town and to drive customers to sign up. So, I set my prices at ninety-nine dollars for a monthly membership of music lessons even though my competitors were charging $120 and $130. I personally thought it was a *great* price, but I still was met with people requesting deals. Deals for siblings, friends, everything you could imagine.

Even though I thought I was getting a handle on dishing out these deals, a colleague of mine at the time called me personally to explain how important it was for her to put her three sons in music lessons. Not only was that three potential clients, but one of them also wanted two lessons. That's *four* accounts! Waaahooo! The problem was that she wanted a discount. A deep discount but not just any kind of deep discount. She wanted the third son to get a reduced price and the fourth lesson to be almost free. I wanted to tell her that she shouldn't have had three kids if she couldn't afford them, but I instead thought about how talented her kids were. We came to an agreement of charging forty dollars for the those two lessons.

I had made a deal with the devil.

From that point forward, that mom was a monster. Demanding special treatment and consistently complaining about everything. I couldn't believe that I had basically given away our services for free, and all I was met with was more aggravation. Ugh!

Through the years, I've raised my rates from ninety-nine dollars to $140 per month for new customers. My rates for longtime clients have increased by a certain amount each year. Yet and still, the mom who was paying forty dollars has incurred yearly increases, bringing her up to a meager and laughable sixty-four dollars. Her kids will graduate soon. I'd rather age them out as opposed to raising their tuition an additional eighty dollars per month. Mostly, I keep them around as a reminder that I only shortchange myself and my family by not asking for more money. My business and every business can operate without those seeking the lowest prices because there are some people who would rather pay for the best product or service.

Lesson learned: Provide more value to your customers and then charge more than your competitors.

Chapter 15
FAIL, BUT FAIL FAST

According to the Bureau of Labor Statistics, about half of all businesses no longer exist after five years. You might even be one of the lucky one-third of businesses who make it past their tenth anniversary. Those numbers aren't even considering the amount of people who didn't get their businesses off the ground. Most entrepreneurs who have a ton of money but don't know how to run a business simply fail bigger. Yet entrepreneurs who learn from their experiences will always be more resourceful, and they'll *make it happen*.

A cushion of seed money is surely helpful, but we've all seen people squander cash without good direction. The one thing that the surviving businesses did differently was that they adapted their businesses and behaviors based on failure. You see, the average entrepreneur creates a business that they *think* will offer a good product or service, but the business owner is not the consumer and has no clue what customers actually want! Once you get past the fact that people may not even like your idea and probably won't buy into your initial plan, then you can find out what they will actually pay for. Start with their problems and be the one to fix it for them.

> "A person who sees a problem is a human being; a person who finds a solution is visionary; and the person who goes out and does something about it is an entrepreneur."
>
> -Naveen Jain

Hustling straight out of college, I created my first music program hoping to be an overnight success. First, I established my company and made a plan for music lessons in students' homes, but I wasn't set up for success. I was only one employee, and it was impossible for me to teach enough students to make a living while being a single mom of a five-year-old in New York City, hundreds of miles from any friends or family.

The second time I tried to get my music school going and really the first time I truly *dove in* by signing a commercial lease, I had the awesome plan of creating a school where people could come take group piano lessons. I had after all worked previously at group piano schools that were wildly successful in New York City. I would write out the future profits on yellow legal pads. Eight kids in a piano class paying one hundred dollars each per month. A teacher would charge us thirty dollars per class, and I'd be making almost $800 for one class where I didn't have to do a single thing. Yes! It *had* to work!

Except it didn't work.

I guess I should've taken the time to find out what the customers in the area of my location actually wanted. It for damn sure wasn't any group lessons. Find out what the customers in your market want and need. Create that product or service and make it irresistible to the consumer.

Squandering Money

Although the wrong business product, service, or models might be the first mistake that you make when starting a business, I assure you there will be a few flops when determining what to spend your money on. I've spent money on all sorts of useless office products, but the one thing that tends to slap me in the face every once in a while is when I spend money on marketing that doesn't work. I'm a pretty routine type of woman. If I find that my marketing strategies are working, I'll keep using them. But awhile back, I was feeling extra ambitious. I had a little bit more money in my accounts than I'd normally find there, and, as a result, I decided to go big. Well lucky for me, there she was—a big old marketing billboard that had caught my attention. I simply *had* to have my advertisement on the billboard. And, so I did! I paid a few grand to get the advertisement up and going. It was perfect!

The only problem was that it was perfectly unprofitable. We had the billboard up in various places for a few months while I flushed thousands of dollars down the drain. Once I checked out our monthly statistics and realized that not a single one of our new clients had come from that billboard. I was mortified. Did I really just spend thousands of dollars on something that got me zero in return? Yup.

I may not have gained a client, but as I have since learned, I "bought knowledge." I now know how *not* to market my business and not to spend a bunch of money testing out new marketing. **It's okay to fail a lot. Fail fast, then try again.**

Failing Hurts

I'll never forget the first colloquium that I attended in the process of getting my doctorate degree. *You know, the piece of paper that I use less frequently than toilet tissue*? I was so excited to be around other like-minded scholars who envisioned solving problems one study at a time. Everyone looked just like me. Bewildered, confused, and exhausted. We all shuffled into the room to quickly hear what our professors had to say. It was that moment that they told us what would be expected of us for the remainder of the doctorate program. It holds true in business every day.

> *"We're going to make you find the hoops. Then we're gonna make you jump through the hoops. And when you get close to the end, we're going to set the hoops that you need to jump through on fire."*
>
> **-unknown**

That phrase spoke to the depths of my soul because every day as an entrepreneur is spent finding a way to solve someone else's problem, making the hard decisions, and literally jumping through hoops. Sometimes things are nice and calm, but other times they're filled with the need to run, jump, and avoid getting burned. Problem-solve your way through failures. Use the information that you learned through your failure as fuel to get the job done and keep getting back up. Every. Single. Time.

I have learned to fail fast and get up again. To keep perspective and not to get too down on myself about all my failed or missed opportunities, I frequently remind myself of the following great words of wisdom. Post them somewhere and remind yourself that failure is evitable but highly useful.

"Tough times never last; tough people always do."
-Robert Herjavec

"You only fail when you give up."
-Naveen Jain

Chapter 16
FULFILL YOUR DREAM WITH INTEGRITY

Once you figure out how to make money, you've got to find a way to hold onto it. People aren't just closing down their businesses because they can't figure out how to sell, they're closing because they couldn't figure out how to protect their empires. No matter how big or small your business is, it's your responsibility to protect it with the proper licensing, insurances, and support through accountants, attorneys, and other necessary professionals. Government agencies aren't the only ones who want a piece of the money pie. Businesses will always be one bad review away from being shut down. Not yours because you're going to protect it.

Brass Balls

Every single day, you've got to have guts. I don't mean to go out and be a jerk to people, but you're going to get tested and have attacks on your business while you're in the learning process. For example, the quality of your service or product may suck sometimes as you're growing. You're going to mess up projects, make the wrong decisions, and possibly lose some friends along the way. That's okay. The guts you'll develop within your first years of business will teach you not to internalize the criticism, to find new ways to get paid, and how to care for your champion customers so deeply that they will refer you to everyone they know.

Inconvenient and Questionable Practices

Every once in a while when I'm in a sketchy deli or watching *American Greed*, I begin to think deeply about the people who recklessly and shamelessly run shady businesses. It blows my mind that these people truly believe that their lack of integrity will never come to light. It always does. If you're starting or operating a business and are considering something that doesn't feel like the right thing, I'm here to beg you to reconsider. Otherwise, people are going to think of your business the way I do about a cute little Mexican restaurant in my town.

It was a Tuesday afternoon, which meant it was my day to cook or order out. I was wiped out, and there was nothing within me that felt like cooking for my family of seven, six of whom are guys. I Googled and found the restaurant online. I was so excited because I remember their Mexican burritos being incredibly delicious but hadn't had them in years. I called up the number on the website and asked them to deliver seven burritos to us. The man on the phone quickly informed me that they don't deliver food after 3:00 p.m. Wait, whaaaaat?! "I'm sorry ma'am, but you can come pick it up from our new location if you'd like," he explained. So, I jumped in my car and made the trip because that Buffalo Chicken Burrito sounded great.

When I arrived, the guy from the phone said, "Here you go, you're all set." I handed him my credit card, and he said, "Sorry, cash only," and pointed to the ATM machine in their lobby. Once again, I'm dumbfounded. They can't spend money to deliver food anymore. They don't take cash (causing me to lose *more* money), *and* they *conveniently* have an ATM there to charge an extra fee just to nail you a little more. Unbelievable.

Now some may think that I'm a little salty because this guy's getting away with a cash-only business, but I've seen the face of an auditor its no fun. The penalties for this would be unbearable and are steep enough to lead anyone into business closure. Not everyone fails to report cash from their businesses, but I've seen horror stories of investigators standing outside of cash-only businesses counting how many people walked in.

The problem isn't running a cash business. Many people run them successfully and with a bit of integrity, although I think there is something to be said for businesses that refuse to make paying easy for clients. The problem is that so many people *pad* their books and truly believe that no one is watching.

It's similar to a restaurant that I love eating at. They have some of the most delicious Caribbean chicken that I've ever tasted. But the first time I read my credit card receipt, I was flabbergasted. Our bill was more than ninety dollars and our tax was less than three dollars. This was in New York City where the tax was 8.875 percent. Something ain't jiving. I felt like someone was going to come grab my food away from me as soon as I tried to take my doggy-bag home because I underpaid. Week after week, the check bills on date night are still low, and I just wonder, how long can this last? Sadly, I have the feeling that I'll have an answer sooner than later. Even sadder, most of these new business owners have no idea that their practices are questionable because they haven't done the research.

This is my plea to the new business owner to understand that everyone is watching! There are so many variables that we can't control. Government agencies, competitors, and obnoxious customers can try to put us out of business, but there are so many things you can do to protect yourself. Be sure that you're doing your part.

- Keep your location clean and safe

- Protect your employees

- Pay your tax bills

- Keep up with legal obligations like permits, etc.

- Charge accurate tax

- Get insurance policies that you need and can afford

- Be reasonable

- Be ruthless

- Donate to your community and causes you care about

- Don't let anyone tell you how to live

Design your own journey and find joy each day with the people you're with.

Think back to when you were a kid. The big question was always, "What do you want to be when you grow up?" Most kids said an astronaut, and I said a singer. But what's the next best thing that most of us weren't even offered as a possibility? Working for ourselves. Being whatever we wanted to be.

I wouldn't trade being an entrepreneur for anything. As I write this final page, I'm sitting on a sweet little patio in Mexico looking out at the beautiful water. The sun is shining down on not just my laptop, but my spirit also because I know my day today is going to be filled with the joy that I have designed for my life.

You have the ability to live out your dream. Work how and when you want. Just make it work for you! If you're willing to offer something great to the world and hustle your butt off to make it a success, then you've already got the game plan that you need. We already spend most of our days thinking through ideas and strategies, so there's no time left to sit on the couch or in your little office planning.

Experience is going to teach you what you need to know. So, get up and be better than you were yesterday. Do the work and be relentless.

Screw the business plan.

Bonus
FINAL PREPARATION

Bonus Chapter
Checklists

Screw the Business Plan is based on the principle that no one should be held up in the planning process, and you should launch your plan into action using skills and strategies that can put money in your pockets sooner than later. What you need instead of a fifty-page business plan is a checklist to get things going. Complete one and move on to the next. Revisit your list routinely, even once your business is running, to make sure you haven't forgotten to keep up with something. Then watch it grow!

Prerequisites

√ Determine what you plan to sell and how you'll profit

√ Choose a name for your business

√ Register your business name

√ Request an EIN

√ Meet with an accountant to choose the best business structure

√ Get all business licenses and permits

√ Cash in on any money you can obtain for launch and your first several months of expenses

- ✓ Begin marketing your business at least three months before launch
- ✓ Set up a website and company email
- ✓ Open a business account
- ✓ Open a merchant account to accept credit cards & ACH
- ✓ Set up social media pages and get followers quickly
- ✓ Begin the hiring process—utilize people you know who could help you get started
- ✓ Test your market and find out if they want/need your service
- ✓ Find a business mentor who can teach you to market your business
- ✓ Get your elevator pitch ready
- ✓ Find online networks of business owners to join
- ✓ Join your local chamber of commerce

The Start-Up Checklist

✓ Hire an accountant to track your profits and losses

✓ Hire a labor law attorney for future staff issues

✓ Choose necessary software

✓ Rent out retail or office staff unless it's a home-based business

✓ Order quality signage

✓ Set up your accounting system

✓ Create a computer database to store contact info of all prospective customers

✓ Hire your first employee

✓ Set up disability, property, and professional liability insurance, workman's compensation, and any other insurances your area requires

✓ Line up your vendors and suppliers

✓ Hold a ribbon-cutting and grand opening

✓ Don't miss calls. Answer business phone early or get an answering service.

New Location Set-Up Checklist

✓ Have a real-estate attorney review your lease

✓ Gain necessary building permits

✓ Have building inspected

✓ Negotiate the lease

✓ Decorate location economically, yet classy

✓ Purchase a decorative item that inspires you

✓ Try to furnish with quality, possibly even used furniture

✓ Set up surveillance of all areas inside and outside

✓ Install phones and Internet system

✓ Secure fire extinguishers and smoke detectors

✓ Install security system

✓ Review safety plan with new staff

Running Your Business Checklist

✓ Check bank account daily

✓ Answer your phones early

✓ Be sure that you have at least twenty different marketing strategies going on at once

✓ Receive daily sales goals/status updates from your head employee

✓ Weekly meetings with employees or one point person

✓ Interview for new employees routinely (before you need them).

✓ Manage social media accounts daily

✓ Follow up with your customers via phone every six months

✓ Audit employee productivity/success

✓ Find a way to go above and beyond for a customer each month

✓ Keep in contact with your accountant, attorneys, and insurance companies to ensure compliance

✓ Order monthly supplies and schedule delivery

✓ Determine your gross sales for the month and year

Sanity and Joy Checklist

✓ Meditate or read affirmations daily

✓ Exercise (even a walk) daily

✓ Schedule weekly activities that you enjoy

✓ Try to read a new book each week or month

✓ Train your staff to make decisions without you

✓ Twice a year, consider how you can afford to hire a new member of your WOW team to free up your time

✓ Schedule travel to a new place each year or just to same place nearby with your loved ones (or by yourself if you prefer)

✓ Buy yourself one expensive item each year to reward your hard work (as long as you're profitable)

Additional Insurance Policies to Consider

... but do not limit them to this list

✓ You should have a **personal umbrella policy** in case you get sued.

✓ You should have **business interruption insurance** in case of floods, natural disasters, etc.

✓ You should have **disability insurance** in case you become disabled.

✓ You should have **wrongful termination insurance** because employees can sue you.

✓ You should have **contingent business income coverage** in case you lose money due to a customer or even a vendor.

✓ You should have **commercial auto insurance** in case you have a business car or send an employee on a business errand and an accident occurs.

About the Author

DR. TALONDA THOMAS is an energetic and highly sought-after speaker, marketing mentor, as well as a business and success coach. She got her start in business at the age of twenty-one, marketing music lessons from her New York City apartment to avoid eviction. She went on to grow a large-scale music school and win national awards for quickly tripling her profits. Dr. Talonda spent ten years teaching in public education before tossing out her six-figure career for an exciting life as a travel-loving entrepreneur. She is dedicated to teaching entrepreneurs how to turn their dreams into sales through simple marketing tools and lifestyle systems that will organize their lives so they can truly live abundantly.

www.ingramcontent.com/pod-product-compliance
Lightning Source LLC
Chambersburg PA
CBHW031618210526
45464CB00004B/1639